Index

Edition Rooth & Stone.
Translation: Catharine Higginson – English.
Graphics: Ola Hollsten, www.kent–ola.se Typefaces: Helvetica.
Copyright © 2021 Edition Hans Rooth
La Bastide HB, Hans Rooth and Lage Stone
ISBN: 978-91-639-7426-7

Introduction

"Let it stand", was the school teachers cry in days gone by for something written on the black-board that was worth remembering and for something that had an important message.

Houses with a history and their interiors, retain their timeless appeal unlike the fast changing trends of today. Their histories become intertwined with the extremely diverse characters who have lived in them and the passing epochs.

Houses tell the story of the people who live or have lived in them, people who have designed or created something or simply made their mark in some way or another. The rooms, contents and decorative schemes showcase the contemporary styles of a particular epoch and together, they combine to provide a lingering taste and scent of a bygone era.

From the baroque architecture of the Cardinal's palace in Avignon to Le Corbusier's humble, wooden 1950's shack outside Roquebrune on the French riviera, to Karen Blixen's childhood home north of Copenhagen, the architectural diversity of the buildings featured in the book is huge. However, all of these buildings are intrinsically linked by their historical importance. In addition, the architecture of the early, expressive modernism of the last century, is the history of today and thus, it is absolutely relevant to re-visit the very interesting buildings from that period.

Large amounts of money and ostentatious display has not always been the driving force behind the construction of the houses in this book.

On the contrary, economic limitations have often created the most personal and functional characteristics. The Zeitgeist can be traced through styles, materials, forms and colours.

The houses in this book are quite randomly chosen and have no homogeneous connection. On the contrary, our intention has been to create a place where all of our many interactions with historic houses and their environments can be housed under the same roof.

Hans Rooth and Lage Stone

WHAT	Copenhagen old Airport terminal
WHEN	1939
WHERE	Copenhagen International Airport, Denmark
WHO	Vilhelm Lauritzen (1894 – 1984)

Copenhagen old Airport terminal

The Danish architect Vilhelm Lauritzen designed the original Kastrup airport terminal, which was inaugurated in 1939. After an intensive lobbying campaign, this architectural masterpiece has been restored to its former glory.
Highly advanced engineering technology and extensive research on details of the original furnishings have resulted in an exceptional restoration project.

Kastrup is one of the world's oldest civil airports and was founded in 1925, close to the city of Copenhagen on the island of Amager. In 1936, The Danish Ministry of transport organised an architectural competition in order to select an architect who would be given the responsibility for the design of a new airport terminal.

Entrants included the renowned architect Arne Jacobsen but the eventual winner was Vilhelm Lauritzen and work began in April 1937.

Vilhelm Lauritzen is regarded as one of the great architects of the Danish modernist movement. Educated at Kunstakademiets Arkitektskole in Copenhagen, he travelled extensively throughout Europe in the 1930s looking for inspiration and was almost certainly heavily influenced by the Stockholm Bromma airport, itself inaugurated in 1936 and one of the new wave of functionalist airports.

Le Corbusier, the Bauhaus school and Frank Lloyd Wright, all architects and schools which foreshadowed and developed the functionalist movement, became role models for Lauritzen. He studied their new construction principles, materials and forms.

The airport construction budget was kept relatively low - 700 000 Danish crowns at the time. To keep building costs down and stay within budget, Lauritzen devised some ingenious solutions. For example, thin floor slats were used as wall coverings and all

the interior partitions are lightweight and moveable. He addressed the cold Nordic weather by supplying the huge window sections with built in heating pipes at the base.

At the inauguration in April 1939, the new airport terminal was an instant success; the overall consensus was that it was a technical masterpiece showcasing the most up to date and elegant design. The future had effectively landed at Kastrup airport.

Ironically, one year later and almost to the day, Denmark was invaded by Germany and the airport was closed to the public.

After the war, Kastrup was still the most modern airport in Europe and began to see increasing air traffic as people were once again free to travel.

In the dazzling white building, over 100 metres long, all the elements work in harmony; the rounded gables, tall narrow columns, projecting roof, the so called "bölgetaket" – a kind of wave like roof construction - and the rows of symmetrical window all work together. The use of materials like teak, stainless steel, Greenland marble and copper, combine to create an elegant and yet stable combination.

Lauritzens building seems to sail, like an elegant Atlantic liner, which references the favoured subjects and ideals of the functionalist era, namely new and faster methods of transport, aviation and aerodynamics.

However, when a new terminal, also designed by Vilhelm Lauritzen, was brought into service in 1960, the old building became sidelined. That followed, there was a constant demolition threat against the building. Thanks to an extensive

and concerted campaign on the part of architects and designers, the plans to demolish the building were eventually overturned and in 1991, the Danish Ministry of Environment declared the air terminal a listed building with the proviso that the building should be moved to another part of the airport.

The then CEO of Copenhagen Airport, Niels Boserup, was an exceptional driving force behind the movement to save the building and can be credited to a great extent with saving the building from demolition.

Moving the building was an exceptional technical feat and took place at night time in September 1999. The entire 2,600-ton, 110-metre-long building was lifted above the ground and put onto trailers.

This meant setting up 50 steel reinforcing structures supported by connected flatbed trucks (with 744 wheels!), along with a procession of bulldozers that were there to clear the runways before the morning traffic began if the building collapsed. Happily they were not needed!

After a year of intense reconstruction and restoration, the air terminal was eventually restored to its former 1939 glory.

The furniture and furnishings are either original pieces or faithful reconstructions and even the crockery, designed specially at the Kongelig Dansk porcelain factory can still be found inside the cupboards in the restaurant.

Today, the old terminal is used to receive heads of state and other VIP arrivals.

WHAT   Djurgården Rowing Club
WHEN   1913
WHERE   Djurgården, Stockholm, Sweden
WHO   Sigurd Lewerentz (1885 – 1975), Torsten Stubelius (1883 – 1963)

Djurgården Rowing Club

In April 1880, on an initiative by a group which included Victor Balck and Hans Naess, the Djurgården rowing club in Stockholm was founded. The first boathouse was built east of an old laboratory building in the Laboratoriehagen area and was inaugurated in 1880. The present boat and clubhouse was designed by the architects Sigurd Lewerentz and Torsten Stubelius and inaugurated in July 1913.

The Royal Djurgården is a vast, green lung, just east of Östermalm district. It is crisscrossed by water and at one point; you can see the inlet which leads to the very centre of Stockholm.

The area is a delightful mix of walking trails which wind through leafy groves of ancient trees and meadows. Along the Djurgårdsbrunnskanalen itself, elongated paths border both sides of the canal.

Several museums, gardens and cafés as well as private homes, add a little touch of classic Stockholm culture; amongst others these include the Wasa Museum, Rosendals Castle, the Thielska Gallery, the Rosendals Trädgård organic restaurant, the Nordiska Museum and the Skansen the open-air museum.

The 1912 Olympic games were held in Stockholm and the boathouse was used as the registration

point for the Olympic rowing and swimming competitions which were themselves held in Djurgårdsbrunnsviken, the idyllic water and canal system close to Stockholm.

The finish line for the rowing competitions was the area by fashionable Strandvägen street by Torstenssonsgatan.

In the same year, the lease on the first boathouse was cancelled due to the launch of a new building project, focusing on the new Diplomatic Embassy area of Stockholm. So, very swiftly, permission was granted to construct a new boathouse to be built in Lidovägen in Djurgården. The boathouse was inaugurated in 1913 and this is the structure which is in existence today.

The timber from the 300 metre long seating gallery built for the Olympic Games at Strandvägen quay, was one of the construction materials used and even today, you can still see seat numbers on the roof. Over the years, the boathouse has undergone carefully undertaken restoration and renovation. Today both the interior and exterior look as they did when the house was built and many of the original furnishings are still in place.

The facade of the boathouse is painted in a light sage green, a shade, which can be seen on many of the old wooden houses in Djurgården. Many of these date from the beginning and middle of the 19th century and some are even older. On the front gate, a blue and white enamel plaque commemorates the year 1880, the year in which the rowing club was founded. Part of the first floor with its long row of small square windows overhangs the ground floor, and thus creates an open, yet sheltered terrace where guests at the café can sit and enjoy a coffee in the sunshine, only metres from the canal. When the large ground floor doors are open, passers by can admire the sleek and elegant boats, both new and old which are stacked along the walls.

The first floor is now a café, furnished with long, communal tables and benches, many of which are original pieces dating from 1913 and which have been treated with boat varnish which gives a perfectly glossy finish. The walls and roof are panelled in pine and decorated with blue and white plaques from rowing competitions dating from the 1880s.

By the start of the 21st century, the sheer number of new boats meant that more accommodation was required, so a new boat shed designed by the architect Gunnar Mattsson, and built close to the old boathouse, was inaugurated in 2004. During the last twenty years, the club has won 22 Swedish championships, with rowers from the club representing Sweden internationally and becoming crowned Nordic senior masters once and Nordic junior masters an amazing six times.

The boathouse is of great cultural and historical value and it is now a classified building, where no alterations may be made without permission.

Villa Eileen Gray

When in 1926, architect Eileen Gray bought
a plot of land in the name of Jean Badovici,
who was an architect and editor, she began
a design and construction project which
would become a super modernist icon.
The plot was in Cap Martin, Roquebrune,
on the French Côte d´Azur.

WHAT	Villa E-1027
WHEN	1926
WHERE	Cap Martin, Roquebrune, France
WHO	Eileen Gray (1876 – 1976)

Today the Villa E-1027, which is open to the public, has undergone an extensive (but as yet incomplete) restoration, but for many years the villa was forgotten, abandoned and became extremely dilapidated, with even the furniture being stolen.

These days pine trees grow in front of the villa and lovely as they are, they detract from the uninterrupted view of the Mediterranean, which Eileen Gray loved so much. Her aim was for the house to give an impression of being akin to a white elegant cruiseliner, sailing out onto the azur blue sea.

The basic architectural structure of the Villa is Eileen Gray's own design; however it was designed in conjunction with her then partner and friend Jean Badovici.

The work was carried out between 1926-1929 and it cannot have been a simple project; the plot is situated in an isolated and rocky part of the region. There are no roads, merely a narrow path, leading up from the train station of Roquebrune.

Eileen Gray (1878-1976) was born in Ireland into a wealthy family and decided to study painting at the Slade School of Art in London, before moving

The name of the house, E-1027
is a cryptogram, devised by Gray:
E is for Eileen, the 10 is for Jean (10th letter),
the 2 is for Badovici (second letter) and
the 7 is for Gray (seventh letter).

to Paris to continue her studies and finally settling there. She became interested in interior decoration and furnishings and discovered a special interest in intricate lacquer work. She went on to learn the technique herself and under the tutorship of lacquer master Seizo Sugawara, became almost perfect at the art.

After the First World War she became interested in the art deco movement and began to lean towards modernist design ideas.

Between 1917-1919, she designed an apartment for a wealthy boutique owner in Paris, Mme Levy, completely with furniture, carpets and lamps. It was for this apartment, that the famous Bibendum armchair was created. The structure was in chrome finished steel with the upholstery in cream leather. The famous chromed steel and glass table E-1027 were also designed for the apartment.

Both pieces of furniture were inspired by the recent tubular steel experiments undertaken by the architect Marcel Breuer (1902-1981) at the Bauhaus School in Germany. The Bibendum chair proved to be a great success and was hailed as a "triumph of modern living".

The income from her work on the apartment made it possible for Gray to open a small boutique /design shop in Paris, in the rue Jean Desert, where works by both herself and friends were available for purchase.

Being both female and a self taught architect, Eileen Gray was considered an oddity in the design world and was evidently ahead of her time.

She was attracted to both Le Corbusier and the Bauhaus school and their philosophy in terms of using new and innovative new materials and construction methods.

As a part of this almost entirely male world, it must have proved challenging at times for Gray, working as she did almost entirely alone, whilst studying, trialling and developing new ideas. The Villa E-1027 is a testament to her abilities and her capacity to overcome the hurdle of working in isolation. It is also a testament to modernity and shows her interpretation of the new architectural ideals of simplicity and practical functionality, with airy, light and uncluttered interiors.

The layout of the house is rectilinear and the structure is flat-roofed with floor-to-ceiling and ribbon shaped windows. The open flow between the living areas is clearly visible.

A spiral staircase descends to the guest room. Another, narrow staircase leads to the servant's room on the ground floor; the door has a lock, which can be left open or closed thus indicating whether the owners wish to be served or not. One third of the house rests on pillars, thus creating a cool, shaded exterior space for the hot Mediterranean summer days.

The furniture, carpets and light fittings, were all especially designed for the villa, but sadly everything disappeared, being either stolen or dispersed during the period of neglect from the 1990s onwards.

Gray had an amazing empathy for the design of intricate and yet highly functional storage. The cupboard doors were all marked with their intended use and storage for clothes, bags, hats and books was all made to measure.

Every possible space has been designed to be as practical as possible, especially in the smaller areas.

Sliding doors, or for example, the opening into the tiled shower room with no door at all, maximise space. The rectangular shaped living room was divided into different zones within the open space, all of which were destined for different purposes, entertaining, resting or reading.

During the restoration project, the team attempted to identify the original colour scheme, and decrying the idea that the modernist movement was always based around white, some traces of colour were found and these reflected Gray's personal

favourites, black, white and beige, an elegant and muted colour palette.

Despite the extensive damage that occurred to the original floor and wall tiles during the forgotten years, enough of the originals remained for the restoration team to commission new copies and these can now be seen on the terrace in front of the Villa.

The small kitchen, which is connected to an outside scullery, sits at the back of the house and the bathroom has been furnished with a similar kind of bathtub to that which would have been found in the property originally.

On the west-facing gable, there is a narrow staircase leading up to a dinky balcony. A wrought iron gate sits in the middle of the stairs; Eileen Gray was not fond of dogs and she probably wanted to stop wild dogs from climbing the stairs.

The solarium, close to the staircase is designed to resemble a small square swimming pool with brown and white ceramic tiles.

It was intended for sunbathing and there is there is an original black and white photo, showing Le Corbusier sunbathing, stretched out in the solarium, but it was also frequently used as a gathering area during cocktail hour

Le Corbusier was a close friend of Jean Badovici and came to stay as a guest during various periods between 1937 and 1939. During the visits he painted ten colourful murals on the white walls, which left Eileen Gray furious; she regarded his murals as a complete intrusion at the

villa, and following on from that, the relationship between Le Corbusier and Eileen Gray became glacial, with Gray finally leaving the Villa and embarking on a new construction project of her own in 1932. Le Corbusier however, stayed on in the area and eventually went on to build his own little summer shack, Le Cabanon, just a few metres from the Villa.

Jean Badovici died in 1956 and with his only legal heir, being his sister who was both a nun and resident in Romania, the house was put up for sale.

Le Corbusier initially wanted to buy the house but was then prevented from doing so; instead, he asked a friend

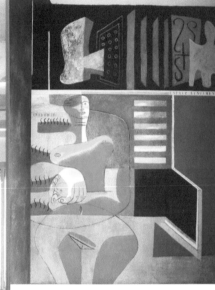

"A house is not a machine to live in, it is the shell of man, his extension, his release, his spiritual emanation"

Eileen Gray

of his, a Swiss national, to buy the place, which she did.

The new owner lived here for several years and made minimal changes to the interiors. After her death, the property was sold again and this time, the new owner occupied the house until his untimely death in the early 1990s, at which point the house fell into neglect. By the end of the decade, it was clear that something needed to be done and in 1999, the Villa was declared a Monument Historique and came under the care of the Littoral.

Later still, the cultural organisation, the Cap Moderne, took on the Villa, Le Cabanon and Tomas Rebuatos' former restaurant the Etoile de Mer, with the remit to restore, maintain and manage the buildings. All of these buildings are now open to the public and restoration work is undertaken as required on an ongoing basis.

The Eileen Gray furniture collection is still sold at the Aram design shop in London. Aram holds the worldwide license for Eileen Gray Design.

Due to the English design buyer, Zeew Aram, many of Eileen Gray's works were put in production in the early 1970s, a few years before her death (1976).

Thanks to Zeew Aram, his Eileen Gray furniture donation to the Villa and Cap Modern, brings new life to the interiors of Villa E-1027.

www.capmoderne.com

Badia a Coltibuono

What a combination! A monastery dating back a thousand years, stunning
Chianti wines, a dedicated family owned and run business, a garden from
the Renaissance, and a prestigious cooking school.
We visit Badia a Coltibuono, one of the oldest wineries in Chianti, high up
on a mountain, at an altitude of 650 meters, in the solitude that can be
found in some of the more isolated parts of Tuscany.

The name Badia a Coltibuono in Latin; "Coltus boni" can be translated as 'good culture, good harvest', an axiom that embodies both meaning and a sense of obligation. The monastery which is more than 1000 years old, was founded by Benedictine monks from Vallombrosa.

From its humble beginnings as a simple church in the Middle Ages, the estate grew and expanded and into something which became well known for its wealth.

Today the monastery is better known for its cookery school, vineyard and olive oil. The estate is owned and managed by the Stucchi Prinetti family with Emanuela and her brothers acting as 'front of house'. They can trace their ancestry back to the Florentine Medicis and the family name is also associated with the manufacture of cars, motorbikes and bicycles, an activity that started at the end of 19th century and continues today.

More recently, Emanuela's mother, Lorenza de Medici di Ottajano Stucchi Prinetti has become a worldwide household name following the publication of her numerous cookery books. She has also become famous in America through a series of Italian cookery television programs which began in the 80's. Lorenza was the founder of the gourmet cookery school in Badia a Coltibuono, which she began with the aim of highlighting classical Italian home cooking. Today the school is run and managed by Emanuela, who is also responsible for the PR and marketing.

The monastery's 800 year history came to an abrupt end when emperor Napoleon I of France annexed Italy, dissolved the monastery and scattered the monks. In 1846 it was purchased by a family who wanted a summer residence; the current owners are their descendants.

Entry is via a small bell, next to the wooden doors which leads to the paved courtyard where the Renaissance architecture meets that of the Middle Ages.

The inner courtyard is at the centre where all the buildings converge.

Despite numerous renovations to the monastery throughout the years, the church and tower are still almost intact and in their original forms.

The entrance to the Renaissance garden and vegetable plot, is also visible from the courtyard.

These were both restored in the 1850's with the original spirit of the gardens being faithfully recreated. Box hedges in labyrinth shapes, lemon trees in old terracotta pots, lavender and kumquats with citrus fruits abound. Roses, irises, and swathes of rhododendrons flower throughout the various seasons. The sweet and tasty "Uva Fragola" – the strawberry grape, covers the pergola near the garden just as it did when the monks were in residence. It was the monks who introduced the San Giovese grape to Tuscany, and this is the grape which is still used in the wine production on the estate today.

The guest bedrooms are located on the second floor. When the building was a working monastery, these rooms were private quarters for certain members of the order. The bedrooms are generous with views over the forest and garden. The owner's private quarters are located in the former kitchen, dining room and huge sitting room which has paintings on the walls and ceiling dating back to the 15th century.

www.coltibuono.com

WHAT   Rungstedlund Museum
WHEN   Dates back to the 16:th century
WHERE   Rungstedlund, Strandvejen, Denmark
WHO   Karen Blixen (1885 – 1962)

Karen Blixen

When Karen Blixen returned to Denmark in 1931
from her coffee farm in Kenya, she moved into the
family residence, Rungstedlund with her mother,
Ingeborg Dinesen, The property is a former tavern,
over the years it has been enlarged and extended
and by Blixen's childhood had become a large,
elegant mansion-farmhouse.

Rungstedlund was purchased by her father, Wilhelm Dinesen in 1879.

Blixen grew up here with her parents, four siblings and numerous servants: chamber maids, gardeners, valets, chauffeurs and grooms.

Today, the oldest part of Rungstedlund dates from 1680 and it was around this time that the property also became an agricultural estate. Blixen herself knew that the mansion could trace its origins back to the 16th century, "Here Rungstedlund stands, where people have been living for hundreds and hundreds of years". Evidence of this is provided by the presence of a 'Runestone' in the park.

During the reign of the Danish king Christian II (1481-1559), 'Runstii Kro' gained tavern status. The estate dates back to 1520 and the Swedish warrior King Charles XII, is said to have been a guest, when he landed at Humlebaek village in 1700.

"The house itself has certainly never been scheduled or designed by an architect. It has grown by it´s own and and has been beautified from time to time, following the taste of new generations"

Karen Blixen

The famous Danish poet Johannes Ewald also lived at Rundsted Kro for periods between 1773-76 and the tavern finally closed in 1803.

Karen Blixen's office was called 'Ewalds stue' - Ewalds room. Karen's style was distinctly 'Scandinavian' when it came to interiors. She was slightly bohemian, although very aware of her aristocratic heritage, fond of light colour schemes and wanted to bring the light inside. As a result, when her mother died, Blixen changed a lot of the interior colour schemes which had previously tended towards the dark and heavy.

Contrary to popular belief, Karen Blixen did not begin her writing career seated in a safari chair in Africa, bashing away on a Remington typewriter, but at Rungstedlund, in the room known as 'Ewalds Stue', a room which had previously been used as an office by her father, the captain and author Wilhelm Dinesen. Her capacity for rich

A veranda with simple rattan chairs faces the park. The office, living room and dining room are on the ground floor along with the 'den grönne stue' or green room, another office room.

Three beautifully hand-carved 'settle' chairs dominate the green room. They were made at Mattrup manor, where Karen's mother Ingeborg grew up. Most of the rooms are en suite here and are all painted in a mild sage colour or in a pale grey shade, except for the 'green' room, which is painted a bright emerald.

During the summer seasons, Karen frequently invited fellow writers to stay in the green room; a kind of artists in residence scheme, where young authors could stay for free.

Karen liked to entertain in front of the big marble fireplace. The window curtains, which flow out onto the floor in the dining room, are probably a referen-

fantasy, her ability to recall detailed memories and her enchanting method of self-expression, was to become her financial salvation after the economic catastrophe that befell her coffee farm in Kenya.

Her father's office chair became Karen's writing chair. Ewalds Stue, is the only room furnished with objects, furniture and paintings from her years in Africa. Masai spears and rifles decorate the wall behind a bookshelf and above her father's gun cupboard, hangs a 'feather' duster made from zebra hair.

During her teenage years in Copenhagen, Karen Blixen attended the Royal Academy of Arts. One of her subsequent works is an oil of a hornbill bird, painted during her time in Africa and given as a gift, to the love of her life, Denys Finch Hatton, an English aristocrat and big-game-hunter.

Blixen's austere bedroom lies on the second floor, looking towards the Rungsted marina with clear views of the Swedish west coast.

ce to the great Danish manor house tradition. Karen had visited many of these houses as a young girl and these extended curtains were to be found everywhere in the Danish mansions and castles of the time. They were a means to display family wealth; the implication being that the family had no need to trim the fabric but rather, could afford to 'waste' it.

The living room has several seating areas. There are magnificent cast iron stoves in almost every room. These were gifts from Blixen's relatives during the 50's. The stoves come from various different Danish manor houses; when the houses were being renovated, the stoves were often replaced with something more modern, discarded and

stored in the attics. When Runstedlund underwent a period of renovations during the 60's, Karen made sure that the stoves found a new home and once re-installed, they proved invaluable during the extremely cold winters.

Blixen loved beautiful flower arrangements and felt that the art was akin to painting. Every year the museum recreates her arrangements with flowers from the Rungstedlund garden.

Karen Blixen on Rungstedlund:
"The house has never been planned or designed by some famous architect. It has grown by itself and has been made more beautiful time and time again, according to the tastes of new generations".

Danish Academy: Karen Blixen was one of the founders of the Danish Academy in 1960. Meetings were held at Rungstedlund, followed by dinner in the dining room. Tables were laid with linen cloths, silver candlesticks and flowers from the garden.

www.rungstedlund.dk

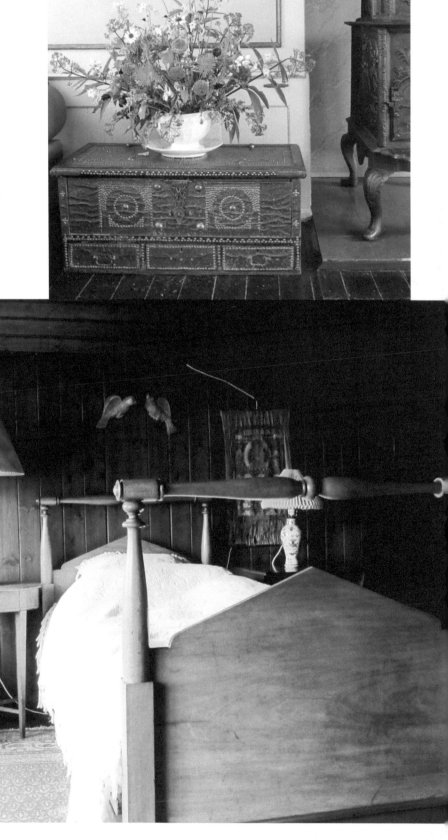

WHAT	The Bauhaus Dessau Building
WHEN	1925-1926
WHERE	Dessau, Germany
WHO	Walter Gropius (1883 – 1969)

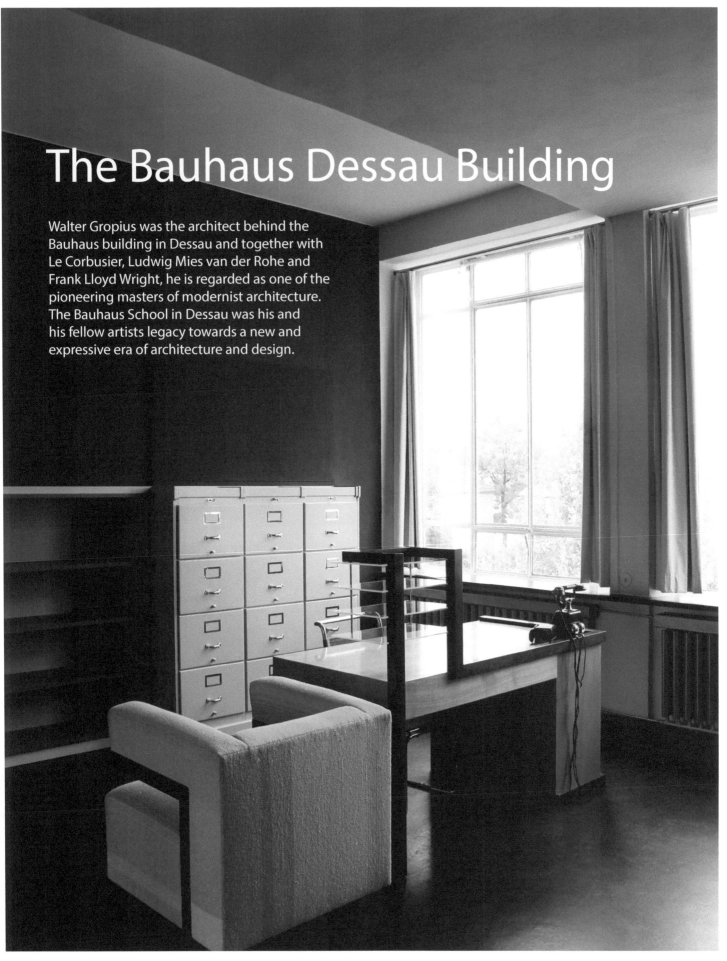

The Bauhaus Dessau Building

Walter Gropius was the architect behind the
Bauhaus building in Dessau and together with
Le Corbusier, Ludwig Mies van der Rohe and
Frank Lloyd Wright, he is regarded as one of the
pioneering masters of modernist architecture.
The Bauhaus School in Dessau was his and
his fellow artists legacy towards a new and
expressive era of architecture and design.

Gropius became an architect just a few years before the outbreak of WW1. He never learned to draw however, and was thus dependant on collaborators, partners and interpreters throughout his career.

In 1908, he joined the architectural practice of the architect and designer Peter Behrens (1868-1940). Behrens, who had begun as a painter, eventually went onto become one of Germany's most influential 20th century architects, and played a vitally important role in the Modernist movement. At the practice, Gropius collaborated with architects which included Ludwig Mies van der Rohe and Le Corbusier.

Two years later in 1910, Gropius established a practice in Berlin together with the German architect Adolf Meyer(1881-1929), and in 1911 the team designed parts of, what was to become regarded as the first modernist building, the Fagus-Werke factory premises in Alfeld-an–der-Leine.

The shoe lasts factory was built in steel and glass, thus breaking totally with tradition. The Fagus-Werke building is now a Unesco World heritage site.

In 1919 Walter Gropius founded the Bauhaus design school in Weimar. It was a completely new type of design school with its aim being to integrate all the different strands of the artistic media of the new modernist era within the teaching syllabus; these included fine art, industrial design, graphics and typography, interior design (textile, glass, ceramics) painting and architecture.

In 1924 the school moved from Weimar to Dessau with the city of Dessau providing funding for the new school building. Gropius designed the building together with colleagues from his private architectural practice.

Very quickly artists and architects flocked to join Gropius at the Bauhaus. Among them were the

architects Marcel Breuer and Ludwig Mies van der Rohe, painters Kandinsky and Paul Klee, textile designers, photographers and glass, metal and wood workers. Anni and her husband who specialised in glass, metal, wood and photography, Josef Albers the photographer and the painter László Moholy-Nagy, as well as the ballet, costume design and graphic artist Oskar Schlemmer.

Together this group formed a melting pot of new thoughts, ideas and ways of working, breaking with the traditional design hierarchy, yet often acknowledging the influence and importance of the Arts and Crafts movement. Their goal was for new creative influences to be integrated into and taken on by the modern, industrialised society that was developing following on from WW1.

At the Bauhaus project, Gropius refined the architectonic ideas he had put into the Fagus-Werke building prior to WW1.

In Dessau as in Alfeld, the glass curtain wall suspended in front of the load-bearing framework defines the exterior of the workshop wing and openly reveals the constructional elements.

He consistently separated the parts of the Bauhaus building according to their functions. The different wings were asymmetrically arranged according to their purposes. The visitor has to move around the building in order to gain an idea of the architecture as there is no central viewpoint.

The main elements of the building are the three-storey workshop wing, the block for the vocational school with its unostentatious rows of windows and the five storey-studio building with its conspicuous, projecting balconies are A single-storey building with a hall, stage and refectory,

connects the workshop wing to the studio building.

The facade of the students' dormitory is punctuated in the east by individual balconies and in the south by long balconies that continue around the corner of the building.

Buildings for masters and teaching staff were constructed close by and designed in tune with the new functionalistic ideas, all corresponding with the Bauhaus ethos.

The entire complex is rendered and painted in mainly light tones, creating a contrast with the dark window frames. In comparison, the interior has a detailed colour scheme, aimed to accentuate the construction of the building.

The Bauhaus design school was closed in 1932 after coming under heavy pressure from the National Socialists and the building suffered

Today, once again, the Bauhaus functions as a vitally important centre for experimental design, research and teaching. It is intrinsically linked with the Bauhaus legacy, dedicated to working on contemporary urban issues.

www.bauhaus-dessau.de

extensive bomb damage towards the end of the war, but was later patched up. In 1974 it was designated a protected monument and was comprehensively restored for the first time in 1976.

The Bauhaus Dessau, created in 1987, became the Bauhaus Dessau Foundation and was declared a World Cultural Heritage Site in 1996. The total restoration was finished in 2006.

WHAT   Le Cabanon
WHEN   1952
WHERE   Roquebrune – Cap-Martin Côte d´Azur, France
WHO   Le Corbusier (1887 – 1965)

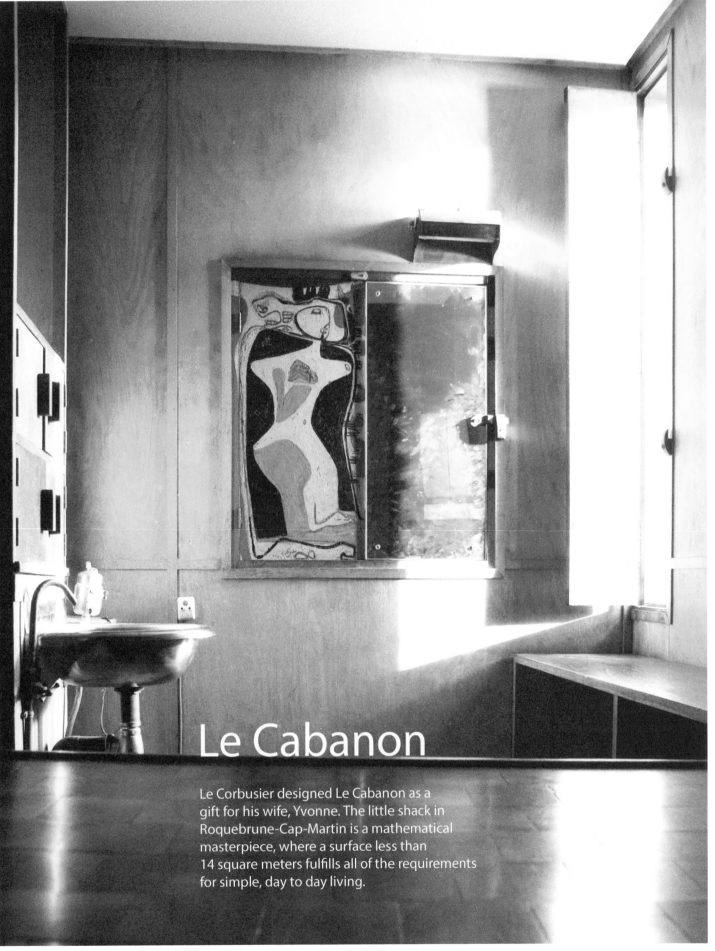

Le Cabanon

Le Corbusier designed Le Cabanon as a gift for his wife, Yvonne. The little shack in Roquebrune-Cap-Martin is a mathematical masterpiece, where a surface less than 14 square meters fulfills all of the requirements for simple, day to day living.

The Mediterranean, the surrounding landscape and the light, proved a powerful draw for French architect Le Corbusier.

In the late 40's, he bought a tiny piece of land on a rocky hillside near the little summer resort town of Roquebrune. The view from here, over the Mediterranean is stunning. The vendor was a Thomas Rebutato, a local craftsman and self taught amateur artist.

Rebutato had built a simple little restaurant, the Etoile de Mer, which, when it opened did not even have running water. Corbusier was one of the very first guests and the men went on to forge a lifelong friendship.

Just opposite stands the iconic house of renowned architect Eileen Gray, the Villa E-1027, designed by her, for herself and partner Jean Badovicci.

Le Cabanon measures exactly 3.66 x 3.66 sq m with a height of 2.26 meters. This measurement is designed to comply with Corbusiers "Modulor" principle; his own calculated measurement system, based upon an average human height (with raised arms) of 183 cm.

With Le Cabanon, Le Corbusier transformed his measurement system into a micro dwelling for himself and his wife.

With a minimum of space, multiple functions interact together in an area hardly bigger than a normal tool shed.

Le Cabanon consists of a work space, a rest area, a wash basin, a table, a coat rack and a wardrobe. Yvonne's bed has a 'repose-tête', a wooden bed head, whose design recalls the severe and minimalist lines of a Japanese sleeping cushion; wooden boxes provide under bed storage.

Lightweight wooden cubes work as small stools and are easy to move around; the wooden knobs are well defined and function as clothes hangers. Small windows placed low down provide light whilst avoiding the harsh glare of the midday sun.

The open plan industrial stainless steel basin provides a clear indication of Le Corbusier's rational approach.

The now faded cupboard fronts were originally painted in bright primary colours, green, red, yellow, cobalt, showing that Corbusier's design palette was not always restricted to white.

The overall extreme simplicity of Le Cabanon contrasts with Corbusier's other works, especially his famous functional villas.

The structure and all of the timber elements were prefabricated at a carpentry workshop in Corsica. The various elements were then assembled on site in Roquebrune, like parts of a Meccano kit.

The facade is composed of vertically placed pine logs, the materials used in the interior are oak and chestnut and the window shutters are made of plywood.

The outdoor 'bathroom' is a simple construction which is a homage to the simple camping lifestyle so popular in and around Le Cabanon.
The shower and a nearby concrete table and stool complement each other perfectly.

A few meters away lies 'Le Baraque'
- the architect's simple studio and workshop built from sheets of corrugated iron. Fig, yucca, agave, pine and eucalyptus trees surround the cabin, creating a perfect miniature natural world at the edge of the Mediterranean.

In July 2016 Le Cabanon was classified by Unesco as a World Heritage Site.

www.capmoderne.com

WHAT   Castle Leslie Estate, Hotel
WHEN   1870's Scottish Baronial style, dates from 1600's
WHERE   Glaslough, Monaghan, Co Monaghan, Ireland
WHO   Samantha Leslie

Castle Leslie

The Leslie family history is a rich mixture of anecdotes and tales of the adventurers, eccentrics and daredevils who made up their number, the royal favours that were bestowed on them, and more than a few ghosts! Castle Leslie has been the family ancestral seat since the middle of the 1600's.

The Leslie family motto, "Grip fast" and its coat of arms, can be traced as far back as 1090, when the then Queen of Scotland, Margaret (1045-93) was forced to flee from a potential Danish occupation. Margaret escaped on horseback and legend has it that she was riding at speed, seated behind her chamberlain, Bartholomew Leslie on his horse, when they were forced to cross a river. Halfway across, the Queen suddenly fell into the water. Leslie quickly took off his belt with its big buckle, lowered it fast flowing river and shouted to his Queen "grip the buckle, fast"!

The Queen later honoured Leslie and it was decided that from here on, the family crest would be an intricately engraved buckle with the motto "Grip Fast".

During the 1660's the Leslie family moved from Scotland to Ireland, and today Castle Leslie in Glaslough, Co Monaghan, stands in extensive parkland. The park is stunning with hundreds of trees, rivers and a lake.

The hunting lodge, itself the size of a large mansion, complete with a beautiful stable yard, stands slightly further away from the Castle.

Whilst construction began in the 1660's, the present castle dates from the 1870's and is built in the style referred to as Scottish Baronial. This is a difficult style to define, especially when it is constructed in an almost 'Tannhüser Like' operatic setting.

During the late 1800's it became an extremely popular building style with European royal families and the nobility as well as rich industrialists, who for the first time, had the means to start building their own stately homes.

The granite facade is somewhat gloomy. True, the different architectural styles that are apparent in the windows, doors and lintels are of interest; however, it is in the stunning interiors, full of family history and carefully maintained as a private home, that the true beauty of Castle Leslie is revealed.

When you enter the foyer, you are immediately made to feel like one of the family and welcomed as such. During the autumn and winter a roaring log fire adds to the cosy feel. One of the more interesting features is the ancient luggage lift which is still in working order and

distributes guest's suitcases to the various floors. There are no such 'mod-cons' for the guests themselves who have to use the stairs!

Here, as a guest, one is immediately welcomed like a family member when entering the foyer. During the autumn and winter seasons, an open fire adds to the cosy feel. A curious technical detail, is the old luggage elevator, which distributes the guest's suitcases to the various different floors. There are no such 'mod-cons' for the visitors themselves - they have to use the stairs!

The guest rooms, drawing rooms, dining room, library and other areas are all decorated with Leslie family memorabilia and personal effects. The colour scheme is quite classic, with a mix of both bright country house co-lours and slightly more faded shades from the late 1800's

such as emerald green, sun flower yellow, bright crimson, pale sky blue and light sage.

Old black and white and sepia photos, often in hand made frames, display a mix of family portraits, famous artists and authors as well as royals, all of whom came on frequent visits to the Leslie´s hospitable and relaxed home. The castle can certainly be said to have numbered a complete cross section of society among its visitors over the years. Perhaps the artistic and bohemian life style combined with the slightly eccentric Leslie family approach, attracted some of the more conservatively brought up guests.

Favoured arm chairs, over-sized beds, dressing tables, delicate little sewing tables, small busts, candle sticks, bookshelves and interesting mementoes from family travels, all mingle together to create a charming and slightly whimsical decorative scheme from days gone by.

The library is full to bursting with ancient leather bound volumes which include biographies, novels and non-fiction, reference works and a wonderful collection of beautifully hand-illustrated first editions on flora and fauna.

The walls are covered with generations of Leslie family portraits whose subjects gaze at the today's guests as they make their way up the stairs. There are endless numbers of interesting busts, crystal chandeliers and small romantic water colours all the way up to the third floor, where the eclectic decorative mix continues in the guest bedrooms.

Samantha Leslie's father, Desmond, was an RAF pilot during WWII; he was also a film director, author and musician and was a pioneer in the electronic music scene. Her aunt, Anita Leslie King, also took part in the war effort, driving ambulances in France. She saved numerous French soldiers behind enemy lines and was twice honoured with the Croix de guerre for her bravery

by President De Gaulle. Samantha's grandfather, Shane, was related to a Winston Churchill via his aunt, Jennie Jerome Churchill.

The huge guest bedrooms are named after family members. The 'Norman' and 'Seymour' rooms refer to two of the sons of Shane and Leonie Jerome and Norman's room is said to be haunted by a ghost. Many of the furnishings are antiques. The canopy bed in 'Norman' dates from 1607. One of the guest rooms has an extremely long bath tub, while another is equipped with a 'seat' style bath.
The bathroom ceramic ware was installed around 1900 and one of the lavatories is equipped with a veritable 'throne', complete with a seat covered in shining mahogany, which is accessed via a few steps.

Castle Leslie is a wonderfully interesting and eclectic family home, and like many stately homes, it is anything but conformist!

www.castleleslie.com

La Colombe d'Or

The village of Saint Paul de Vence in the French
Alpes Maritimes, dates from the early Middle Ages.
Today, it is a 'must see' for all those tourists on the
picturesque French village trail. For those in the
area, the mythical Hotel la Colombe d'Or, which is
about to celebrate its 100th birthday, is well worth
a detour, even if it is only to admire the unique
painitings by numerous artists which adorne its
ancient walls.

WHAT	La Colombe d'Or, Hotel & Restaurant
WHEN	1920 with later alterations
WHERE	Saint Paul de Vence, France
WHO	Paul Roux & family

Paul Roux was the driving force behind
La Colombe d´Or when it started life in 1920 as
"Chez Robinson", a café / bar with an open
air-terrace; people would flock to the impromptu
dances held there at the weekends.

It quickly became quite a draw, attracting all kinds
of interesting 'characters' from the local neigh-
bourhood, so Paul, enthusiastically backed by
his wife Baptistine or 'Titine', decided to extend
and reopen as the Colombe d'Or, an inn with
three rooms.

Paul Roux came from a farming background. However, his abilities as a host combined with his intelligence, good taste, interest in the world at large and a tactful nature, quickly began to attract many of the artists who were staying in and around the area of Saint Paul de Vence. La Colombe d´Or quickly became a magnet for both unknown and established artists.

Paul's deep rooted interest in the arts and the friendly and relaxed atmosphere that pervaded the hotel-restaurant, brought increasing numbers of new artists. The hotel was extended again to cope with the growing demand and soon, the walls were covered in paintings, in both the public areas and the guest bedrooms. Very often these works of art were exchanged against the cost of the accommodation or meals.

Saint Paul de Vence is a beautiful village and as word spread of its beauty, both French and other international celebrities began to come and stay at La Colombe d´Or.

In 1940 the South became part of the 'free France' zone and a large group of philosophers and artists drifted towards the Côte d´Azur, turning the Colombe d´Or into one of the places to meet. Jacques Prevert was a fairly typical example; he lodged at the hotel during the filming of Carnet´s 'Devils Envoys' and somehow never left, subsequently moving to the village and becoming one of Paul´s closest friends.

Painters such as Picasso, Georges Braque and Marc Chagall were also drawn to the hotel. Alexander Calder was a regular and went on to become another of Paul Roux's good friends. His paintings and ironwork sculptures are today an intrinsic part of the hotel's history.

The end of the war saw the arrival of the international crowd.

The 50's was the era of Miro, Braque and Chagall, followed by Cesar and many other illustrious members of the arts scene. The actor Yves Montand and actress Simone Signoret, who

had a little house in the village at that time, met at the hotel and later married in the village church.

Paul´s son Francis and his wife Yvonne went on to follow in Paul´s footsteps, commissioning amongst other works, a ceramic by Fernand Leger for the terrace. The art collection has grown year upon year; the latest work to be installed is a large ceramic piece for the swimming pool area by the Irish artist Sean Scully.

When the Maeght Gallery opend in the early 60's, close to Saint Paul de Vence, it created yet another reason for both established and up and coming artists to visit La Colombe d´Or. Black and white photographic images from the period show the stars of day visiting the hotel for the night or simply lunching with their contemporaries.

From the outset La Colombe d´Or has attracted artists, writers and actors and today, they continue to visit, albeit discretely. Perhaps they appreciate the discretion, enjoy the fact that the hotel is not widely known and wish to keep it that way.

The set up is comfortable, simple and at the same time, luxurious in an understated manner. Rather, the rooms are homely and not overly fussy. Staying here is akin to visiting, if you were lucky enough to have one, your great grandmother's house in the French countryside. As Francis Roux´s daughter in law, Daniele, explains "Perfection would be very boring in a way".

The restaurant area is charmingly old fashioned, elegant and comfortable, with the tables laid with white linen cloths. Beautiful fresh flowers arranged daily are a typical touch in this 'home from home'. From most angles the guests get an overview of the other guests, this creates quiet yet intriguing conversation pieces on the subject of just 'who is who'. Original masterpieces still hang on the walls in every room. Amongst others, guests can enjoy a Calder, a Sonia Delauney, a Picasso, a Doufy, a Braque and a Legér. The artwork really is an integral part of the hotel and as Daniele Roux says, "We never think of the paintings, the walls speak".

At the side of the reception area is a little bar with a few places to sit. This has long been a gathering area for pre-lunch or dinner drinks and non-residents are free to pop in for a drink or a glass of wine. The overall ambience is neither chic nor fashionable but instead charming and unpretentious, a relaxing corner furnished with individual pieces, wooden stools and benches.

The emerald green swimming pool was the first one to be installed in the area in the early 60's. It is overlooked by an Alexander Calder sculpture and placed between traditional neighbouring houses in an outspoken, Italianate architectural style with beautiful colour schemes that have faded over the centuries.

When Paul Roux's health began to detoriate, his wife Titine went to visit Picasso and pointed out that he had never given Paul a painting. She returned with three; presumably both she and Picasso were of the opinion that the numerous lunches and dinners he had eaten at

La Colombe d´Or ought to be finally cashed in. Picasso attended Pauls funeral in person, clearly demonstrating his regard both for the man and La Colombe.

www.la-colombe-dor.com

WHAT   Unité d´Habitation
WHEN   1947-52
WHERE   Marseille, France
WHO   Le Corbusier (1887 – 1965)

Unité d´Habitation

The need for the construction of new residential buildings,
above all for the masses, became a rallying cry in post-war
Europe. Le Corbusier's apartment block, the Unité d´Habitation
or 'HousingUnit' - was built in Marseille between 1947-52.

The need for the construction of new residential buildings, above all for the masses, became a rallying cry in post-war Europe. Le Corbusier's apartment block, the Unité d´Habitation or 'HousingUnit' - was built in Marseille between 1947-52. With its utopian design for city living, it became seen as an ideal standard for the new era of apartment block construction that was taking place all over the world, despite some complaints from detractors who complained that the children's rooms were small and some rooms lacked windows.

Le Corbusier's social planning ideas for an urban community were made flesh with the 12 storey building in the centre of Marseille, the Unité d´Habitation. Constructed in rough cast concrete, the building provided accommodation for 1600 people in 337 apartments. This style which became know as 'brutalist concrete' went on to flourish and become a role model for the massive building boom of the 50's and 60's in Europe.

Although it was not always recognised as such, the Unité d'Habitation was actually an example of Le Corbusier's radical social thinking on employment, utility and function. Along with the maisonette apartments, the building also contains a hotel, a school, chapel, library, childcare and medical facilities as well as shops and restaurants. The roof terrace holds a paddling pool and running track and residents can also enjoy the unobstructed views over Marseille and the Mediterranean.

The Unité, which was also referred to as a "vertical garden city", became Le Corbusier's first large scale project. Then as now, land was expensive so he got around this problem by building high. His overriding aim was to focus on the interaction between public and private spaces. He wanted to link the private apartments with the social areas where people could shop, eat, exercise and mingle and as a result, the Unité is very different from his other residential projects for private individuals.

As often seen in Le Corbusier's projects, he focuses on function, effective execution and practical details. The building rests on columns above the ground, thus creating important airflow. The relatively small maisonette apartments feel spacious and lofty thanks to adequate headroom. Here again Le Corbusier based his spatial calculations on his own so called 'Modular' method, a system built around human body height.

The sliding doors between the rooms are an efficient use of space and the perforated concrete balcony walls provide much needed airflow. This helps circulate air within the apartments when the balcony doors are open and Le Corbusier's use of bright, primary colours on the balconies liven up the grey concrete facade.

"The materials at city planning are: sky, spaces, trees, steel and cement; in that order and that hierarchy"

Le Corbusier

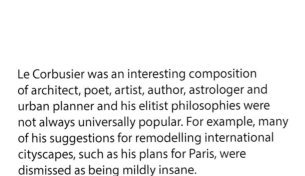

Le Corbusier was an interesting composition of architect, poet, artist, author, astrologer and urban planner and his elitist philosophies were not always universally popular. For example, many of his suggestions for remodelling international cityscapes, such as his plans for Paris, were dismissed as being mildly insane.

However, the Unité, which, when it was constructed was clearly way ahead of its time, can be seen as an example of architectural social reform, almost like a 'kolchos' (collective farm), a city within the city, a gathering place and a resting point right in the centre of bustling Marseille.
This is a tower block, where the turquoise rooftop pool and its stunning views, helps the area act as the traditional village 'market square'; a gathering place, not unlike the piazzas of the Middle ages.

WHAT   Bröndums Hotel
WHEN   1840
WHERE   Skagen, Denmark
WHO   Erik and Anna Bröndum

Bröndums Hotel

Skagen, Denmark's most northerly outpost, is known
for its outstanding light, which was immortalised by the
famous Skagen school of painters. Almost as famous,
is the Bröndums Hotel, where the artists stayed and
socialised during their visits to Skagen.

During the latter part of the 19th century, artists came to the little fishing village of Skagen where the Kattegatt and Skagerrak straits meet. They came to paint the famous light, the sea and the sky. But they also came to depict everyday life in the very simple village.

Over time Skagen became a popular resort for celebrities such as the authors Hans Christian Andersen and Karen Blixen and King Christian X of Denmark.

Bröndums hotel was a particular draw. The long trip from Copenhagen must have been exhausting in times gone by, when guests had to come by horse and carriage, often over the dunes with no proper road.

It is claimed that Karen Blixen wrote parts of her book 'Out of Africa', during some of her numerous visits to Bröndums and a room, simply furnished

with twin beds, an old writing desk, a couple of chairs and blue flowered wallpaper has been dedicated to the famous writer

Bröndums hotel is undoubtedly the central point of Skagen. For over a century, the village has welcomed guests from all over the world who either come to stay or just to visit the famous watering hole of the Skagen painters. Despite numerous extensions to the building itself over the years, a great deal of the interiors are original dating from the 1890s or earlier.

The entrance is simple with an old fashioned reception desk; from the moment you arrive you feel transported back to a bygone era. The high ceiling has dark panelling and a narrow staircase leads up to the guest rooms. To the right of the reception is the breakfast room, originally built as a holiday apartment for King Christian X of Denmark.

The Bröndums hotel was run like an "enjoyable family by an enjoyable family", says the hotel´s CEO. The entire family, Erik, Anne and all their children lived in one of the hotel´s extensions with a bedroom each. There was a general store on the ground floor together with the private hall where guests were served breakfast.
The guest rooms were very simple.

To the right of the reception lies what has to be called the heart of Bröndums, the beautiful dining room. In the olden days, this airy porch like room was used as a guest drawing room.

The dining room was totally restored in 2008, in a simple but elegant manner with dark mahogany furniture and whitewashed pine flooring and the tables are laid with starched white linen.

The different drawing rooms are elegantly furnished in different styles from the 19th century with the walls painted in elegant colours like sage and curry. The main drawing room, situated in one of the extensions, is in the Biedermeier style with sofas, chairs, wall clocks and mirrors, and walls painted in ice bluce

Bröndums hotel was opened in 1840 by Erik and Anna Bröndum. Their daughter Anna, one of six siblings, went on to become a skilled painter and married her colleague artist, Michael Ancker. Young Michael came to Skagen during the summer 1874 and he and Anna became the lynchpin of the famous artists´colony.

As a Crown Prince, King Christian X of Denmark, often came to Skagen and got to know the Bröndum family well. After a timid request from the Prince, the Bröndums had a "ferielejlighed" – holiday apartment, specially built for the royal guest. As King, Christian continued to visit regularly, often with his consort, Queen Alexandrine. The usual protocol was that a couple of days before-hand, there would be a polite phone call from the court in Copenhagen requesting the possibility of a royal visit? This very popular and 'no frills' royal couple, became close friends with the innkeeping Bröndum family.

The artists staying at Bröndums frequently wrote to family and friends praising the quality of the food; fresh oysters and lobsters were often on the daily menu.

Mr Bröndum himself would go out hunting partridge and snipe when they were in season and these would be later prepared in the kitchen by Mrs Bröndum with the help of a maid. Bröndums has

never been known as an extravagant place but the focus has always been on good food and today, the restaurant kitchen produces typical Danish traditional fare, infused with a modern touch. Meals are served on beautiful Royal Copenhagen Porcelain plates with the famous "Musselmalet" design.

Bröndums is well situated in the middle of the old town with its picturesque houses. Skagens Museum is just a short walk away and it is worth visiting for its unique collection of works by the Skagen school, which include among others, Anna and Michael Ancher, Marie and Peder Severin Kröyer, Lauritz Tuxen, Viggo Johannsen and Holger Drachmann.

But perhaps the most impressive aspect of the museum is the 'dining room' furnished with all the famous works that were originally hung in the hotel and collected by Dan Bröndum, who donated the entire collection to the museum, which he helped to create.

www.broendums-hotel.dk

Alvar Aalto House

Alvar Aalto was a world famous architect, who frequently worked alongside his designer / architect wife Aino on both interior and architectural projects.

When you reach the address, the first impression is of a discrete facade that appears almost closed to the street. The entrance door is in wood and stands out from the white house.

The harsh and almost strict appearance is striking and contrasts with the irregular slate path that leads to the main door.

In 1936 this modern and functionalist house, situated in a suburb of Helsinki, called Munkanäs, was completed and ready to move into.

The building was one of Aalto's earliest projects, but it shows signs of his eventual signature style with its use of natural materials and timber either on the facade as battens, or within the interior.

Inside the use of timber pillars and exposed framework provides an interplay of light and shadows. The large windows, always a feature of Aalto's work, provide extensive natural light. The living room is spacious, with comfortable furniture for entertaining.

The low shelf under the window, designed for both books and magazines as well as for houseplants, is a notable feature which gives the strict lines of the room a softer touch. The big window is also framed by plants on the outside, which creates the feeling of having the garden almost inside the house.

The house was designed to provide a combination of private living space and an office area together with a studio. The office part of the house is slim and with high ceilings constructed in white brick-work. The windows and their placement provide clear references to the functionalist movement.

The private part has several sections with different volumes, painted in black and overlooking the garden. A section of flat roof provides a large wooden terrace on the second floor.

The living room is the centre of the house, with a dining room and the office part set off it. The office area is accessed by floor to ceiling sliding doors. There are numerous places to sit and relax in the living area along with a discrete built-in fireplace. Space for a large piano reveals the couple's passion for music.

The upper level houses the bedrooms, toilets and bathroom. The overall impression is of sparsely decorated rooms, all furnished with Alvar Aalto's now well-known designs, which had begun to be produced in 1935 by Artek, a company established by Aalto himself, Marie Gullichsen and Nils-Gustav Hahlin.

From their first showing, the furniture designs made a huge impact; the unique forms and production techniques created a contemporary, futurist look and the era of Finnish design was born.

www.alvaraalto.fi

WHAT	Pension Briol
WHEN	1928
WHERE	Italian Tyrol mountains
WHO	Hubert Lanzinger (1880 – 1950)

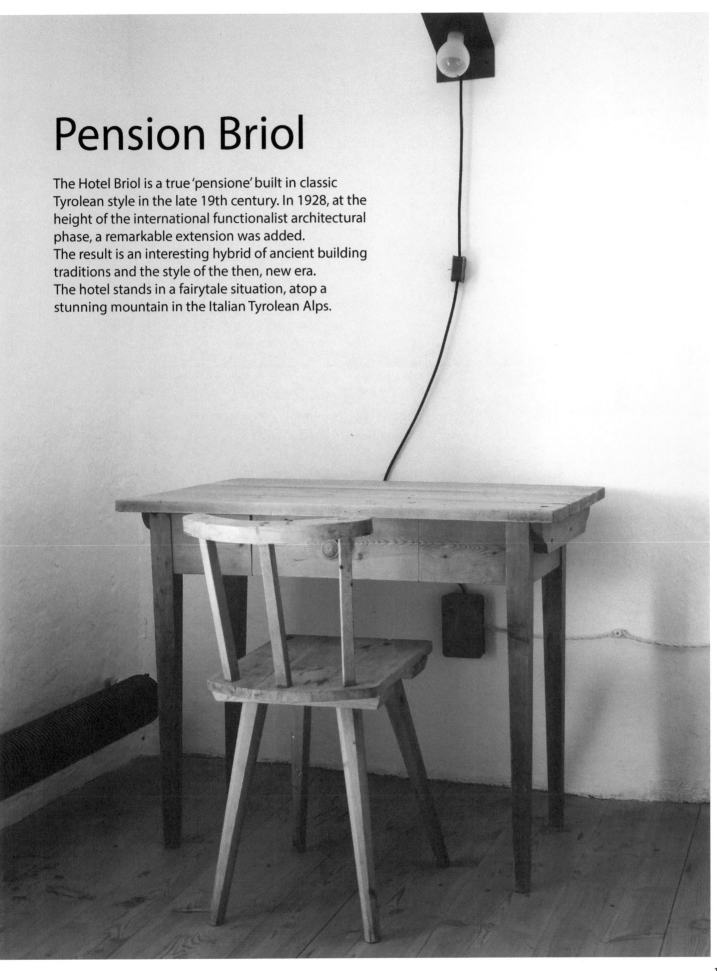

Pension Briol

The Hotel Briol is a true 'pensione' built in classic
Tyrolean style in the late 19th century. In 1928, at the
height of the international functionalist architectural
phase, a remarkable extension was added.
The result is an interesting hybrid of ancient building
traditions and the style of the then, new era.
The hotel stands in a fairytale situation, atop a
stunning mountain in the Italian Tyrolean Alps.

The present owner's great grandmother, Johanna Settari, was just a young girl when she married a silk and china salesman. Despite being a mere street vendor, the bridegroom was a wealthy man and brought a good sum of money into the marriage. The bride was an ambitious and energetic young woman. In 1880, Johanna decided against continuing the (then current) practise of being given a piece of jewellery on the birth of each child and instead, requested a plot of land in the Alps. Johanna went on to have 15 children (11 of whom were daughters) and thus ended up with a considerable chunk of valuable land where she eventually built her first house.

She had four more houses built for her rapidly growing family and in 1898 opened her first guest house. Hiking in the Alps was booming. Guests from all over Europe streamed to the area for their summer vacations; fresh air, exercise and a healthy outdoor holiday had become quite the thing.

"Lanzinger is building a new facade, strongly inspired by the Bauhaus movements functionalistic principals"

The business thrived and when the new functionalist architectural ideas reached the Alps, a decision was taken to extend one of the Settari houses in truly remarkable style. Until 1928 the house had served as an annex to the sister hotel, Dreikirchen, further down the valley. Despite being not universally popular (due to his pro-German nationalist stance), the Austrian artist Hubert Lanzinger was hired to oversee the remodeling project.

He was tasked to design a new facade, strongly inspired by the Bauhaus movement's functionalist principles. The remodeling of the facade and the interiors went hand in hand. A new flat roof and a timber loggia with a view over the valley were also added. Lanzinger paid enormous attention to every individual detail in the new interiors.

The upper parts of the exteriors are covered in vertical timber cladding and the lower levels are in simple whitewashed masonry. The window shutters are painted in olive green and the doors of the main entrance are picked out in a bright lemon green shade.

The result is a notable architectural mix of classic Italian alpine timber construction and a completely plain addition, inspired by the new linear functionalist ideals of the era.

The passage of time has given the building a wonderful patina, the timber exteriors are a beautiful soft grey shade and will continue to age well in the future.

Close by lies the first ever outdoor swimming pool constructed in the Alps which was heralded as a sensation when it was first installed. It is a simple concrete construction which adds to rather than detracts from the mountain setting. It's unheated and is perfect for cooling off in the hot alpine weather during the summer season.

All of the original fixtures and fittings have been kept. The original colour schemes are still in place and the furniture, crockery and glassware is still in use. There are simple pine tables and chairs with communal tables for larger gatherings, decorates with freshly picked alpine flowers. The overall impression is of an orderly, clean, pure and almost 'Calvinist' ambience, lightened by little touches like the fresh flowers.

The guest rooms have neither ensuite toilets nor showers; everything is communal here, facilities are shared, just as in days gone by. Social divides have never been encouraged at Briol and today, passing hikers will be offered a glass of ice cold water from Briol's own spring and a chat with the current owner, another Johanna.

There is no real road to reach Briol. You can either walk up from the nearest railway station (this takes around an hour) or, you can order an 'Alp taxi', a four wheel drive. Alternatively, Johanna, will pick guests up on arrival in the nearest village and return them when they are ready to leave.

Johanna is following her "urgrossmutters" (great grandmother's) fundamental principles in terms of her management of the house and land - simplicity and authenticity.

Don't change, let be.

www.briol.it

WHAT   Hansaviertel housing complex
WHEN   1957-1961
WHERE   Berlin, Germany
WHO   Alvar Aalto, Oscar Niemeyer,
    Walter Gropius and many more

The Hansaviertel

The Hansaviertel housing project in Berlin was completed in 1961 and is an architectural conceptual totality based around the modernist principles of rationality, functionality, space and light. Hansaviertel is a small district between Grosser Tiergarten Park and the Spree River, within the central Mitte borough of Berlin.

Constructed between 1957-1961, the Hansaviertel complex area is a very 'human' settlement with its architecturally diverse and interesting buildings - tower blocks, low rise housing, green spaces and a curvaceous street network.

The project's motto "urban living in a park" reflects the Berliners love of green spaces, most notably the Tiergarten.

The Hansaviertel area had been originally built around 1872. Further development then took place until the early 1900's. Much of the existing housing was built in the beautiful 'Jugend' or art nouveau style and was favored not only by aristocratic Berliners but also by some of the most influential people of the era such as the artist Käthe Kollowitz, the philosopher and revolutionary socialist Rosa Luxemberg and even for a short period, Vladimir Lenin. It was an illustrious neighborhood.

Sadly, in 1943 during some of the heaviest bombing of WW2, Hansaviertel was almost entirely destroyed. Reconstruction was a priority and by 1946 the City Council had already started planning a rebuilding programme. The project was to take the form of a housing estate and the intention was to create a contemporary Hansaviertel using the zeitgeist of modern multiple family unit housing planning. Rationality, clarity, function and 'green lungs' were the keywords.

In 1952, Le Corbusier, Arne Jacobsen, Alvar Aalto, Walter Gropius and Oscar Niemeye were among just some of the renowned architects of the time who were invited to take part in a competition which would decide on the direction of the new zone. They were all keen advocates of "Neues Bauer" or new architecture and this was reflected in their proposals which were all shown at the Interbau 57, a nationwide series of architectural exhibitions. A total of 53 architects representing 13 countries took part.

A final selection of 35 designs was chosen from the various proposals; these ranged from tower blocks to individual family homes and terraced properties. A number of leading landscape architects were also engaged to plan the new green spaces and the project soon became known as an impressive showcase for modern living.

Each and every building displays a degree of individuality with carefully chosen material combinations and well-executed detailing characterizing the build. Sitting amidst the tower blocks, the single family homes have a low key appearance and underline the approach of 'architecture for everyone'. There are views over the green spaces for all residents, whether they are high-rise dwellers or living at ground level. The absence of heavy traffic and the extent of the planting means that the whole project possesses a feeling of tranquility.

Inside the buildings, open plan layouts, modular walls and under-floor heating were both novel and practical design solutions. So too were the children's play areas which were installed on covered balconies.

The central location of Hansaviertel meant that the area was easily accessible from many major routes and despite being in the midst of noisy Berlin, the extensive use of green spaces meant that the area became a veritable city oasis.

The Hansaplatz square contains a shopping arcade, a library still with its original fittings and a theatre. Construction began on an underground station in 1957 and the U9 metro line opened in 1961. The entire Hansaviertel site, including the two churches, has historic monument status and although the design is approaching its 60th anniversary, the visible modernism of Hansaviertel's architecture is still strikingly apparent.

Hansaviertel can be considered an example of extremely well executed town planning where equal importance has been placed on both the 'human' element and the architectural aesthetic.

WHAT   La Mirande Hotel Restaurant
WHEN   1309/1653/1987
WHERE   Avignon, France
WHO   The Stein family

La Mirande

In 1309, the papacy moved from Rome to Avignon. When Pope Clement V arrived here, he was accompanied by one of his nephews, the Cardinal de Pellegru. The Cardinal decided to build his own cardinal palace and today, the Hotel La Mirande, which dates from the 17th century, stands on the site of the ancient cardinal palace.

"The family, passionate about old buildings, had moved from Germany to Provence in search of a classical restauration project. With the discovery of La Mirande, their search ended"

The historic centre of Avignon has seen plenty of Italiante influence over time in terms of its architecture, street layout and open spaces. Clearly, the city's papal visitors have had some degree of influence on its history. The Hotel La Mirande is located opposite the huge 'Palais des Papes' or papal palace and from the hotel rooms and garden, the palace is almost within touching distance.

The original Cardinal's palace was burnt to the ground during a siege of the Papal palace in 1410. The ruins were eventually restored and in 1653, a completely new facade was installed in the contemporary baroque style by architect Pierre Mignard, himself the son of Nicolas Mignard, court painter to Louis XIV.

For over two centuries 'La Mirande' went by the name of 'Hôtel Pamard' and was owned by an eminent local family, one of whom eventually went on to became the mayor of Avignon. During his

time as mayor in the late 1900's, large parts of the
city were renovated, rebuilt and generally brought
up to standard in the style that became known
as 'Haussmann' after the modernisation of huge
swathes of Paris under the auspices of the then
Prefect, Baron Haussmann.

When the current owners took over La Mirande in
1987, they found the gloomy, uninhabited building
in a state of decay. The family are passionate
about old buildings and had moved from Germany
to Provence in search of a restoration project.
Their search ended when they came across La
Mirande and embarked on an extensive renovation
programme that was to last over three years and
result in the recreation of the Cardinal's Palace.

A thoughtful and sensitive approach to renovation
resulted in the restoration of the original facade
and the walled garden. The inner garden was
transformed into a patio area. This was a huge

project, all the daily requirements of a reasonably large hotel had to be addressed, large amounts of equipment had to be sourced and installed and a hi-tech professional kitchen needed to be carefully designed and fitted.

Over three centuries worth of differing architectural styles and interior decorative input had left a mark on all the elements of the building, whether it be the rooms, gardens or terraces. For the owners, it was vital that all of these different elements worked together. The styles of the 17th, 18th and 19th centuries needed to work in harmony. No one era was to be eclipsed by another. The family worked frenetically in order to achieve this delicate balance which has allowed every single room, wall, floor, ceiling, window and door, to express it's individual character from the various different periods. They consulted experts from France, Switzerland, Italy and the UK and engaged local artisans and craftsmen as well as specialists in fields such as textile conservation, ceramics and antiques, to carry out the execution of the project.

They had discovered the remains of some ancient textiles and after careful examination, they were carefully examined and reprinted. Traditional paint techniques were explored to test and then produce 'new' paint shades to match the originals. The furniture was all sourced and purchased at auctions or flea markets. The same applies to the ceramics, mirrors, cutlery and crockery; nothing was left to chance.

The stylish and individual, yet historically respectful interior scheme had finally come together.

With a delicate sensitivity towards the most significant design periods of the 18th century, many of the interior textiles used at La Mirande were inspired by the designs that came from the Far East and China. A large number of these designs were produced at the Royal factury in Jouy, near Versailles during the 1760's, and many of them can be seen at La Mirande today having been reprinted and reissued in special new editions for use at the hotel.

A discrete brass plaque is the only cue to what lies behind the serene baroque facade of the Hotel La Mirande where ancient slab floors, antique ceramics, 18th century walnut, delicate Toile de Jouy and heavy linens combine to create a wonderfully restful interior scheme and where, three centuries of history await the guests.

www.la-mirande.fr

César Maneique was born in Lanzarote in 1919. On leaving secondary school he decided to study technical architecture, in order to better understand the technical constraints of the building process, but abandoned this after a couple of years to move to Madrid to attend the Academia de Bellas Artes de San Fernando, where he eventually graduated as a painter and Professor of Art.

Manrique spent five years living and studying in Madrid before embarking on several trips to Europe and the USA to learn about both classical and modern architecture.

Right from the start, he was determined to work on producing a form of 'quiet' or discrete architecture which could sit in harmony with the natural landscape without disturbing the elements.

Between 1964-66 he lived and studied in New York, in great part due to a scholarship from Nelson Rockefeller, art collector and patron and later vice president of the USA.

When Manrique finally returned to Lanzarote in 1966, he settled down and started to build his first home on the island. He was commissioned to execute several architectural projects and ultimately, had an enormous influence on the local planning and building regulations in Lanzarote.

He was an early and enthusiastic environmentalist and a strenuous champion of low key housing built in a local and traditional style.

All the hotels, which he designed, follow local traditions in terms of both colour schemes and decoration. Manrique's architecture is both playful, organic and almost 'stolid'; the roots can often be traced back to - simple Lanzarote farming culture.

Manrique was instrumental in ensuring that the frequent demands made by the tourist industry for ever higher and increasingly large hotel complexes were rejected. His strong feelings on the subject set the tone for the urban planning policy.

Manrique's first home in Lanzarote was built in 1968 directly onto a volcanic area created by an eruption in the late 1700's.

The ground floor consists of Manrique's several studios and his private rooms.

The style of the house is simple; it is white-washed in typical Lanzarote style, but with a more modern feel, larger reception areas and big windows. The lower floors are built into the volcanic 'bubbles' and thus have a slightly rounded shape which creates a sensational, theatrical effect.

The interiors are executed in typical fashionable 60's style and mainly designed by Manrique himself, assisted by local craftsmen and furniture makers. However, he clearly had his own take on 1960's style.

The colour scheme is bright and creates a strong contrast to the white washed 'bubble rooms' which are situated in what is known as the cellar. There is also a recreational area with a turquoise blue swimming pool, a barbecue and a little dance floor. It is very easy to see the interior as a backdrop for some glitzy Hollywood film from the 60's.

The house has a little plaza with a fountain by the entrance. Cacti and tropical plants in strange formations abound; these were a source of inspiration to Manrique, they also add to the decorative scheme and lend the building the air of a stage set.

In 1982, Manrique, with the support of friends, turned his home into a foundation and it is now a museum. The foundation is a private not for profit organisation and the revenues from ticket sales and the small gift shop go directly to arts and cultural projects in Lanzarote.

Alongside Manrique's own works, famous artists such as Picasso, Miro and Tapiès are also represented in the museum.

César Manrique was always deeply involved in the every-day living conditions of the average man. He was one of the earliest architects to understand the crucial importance of architecture for people; having moved from a traditional village to a modern environment he was able to relate to their surroundings.

New villages have replaced old ones, often in an uneasy symbiosis. In Lanzarote, the transitional complexity of redirecting the old island farming culture, towards mass tourism was counterbalanced by Manrique's draftsmanship and social conscience.

www.cesarmanrique.com

Cèsar Manrique's second and final home in Haria, Lanzarote, is also a museum and can be visited.

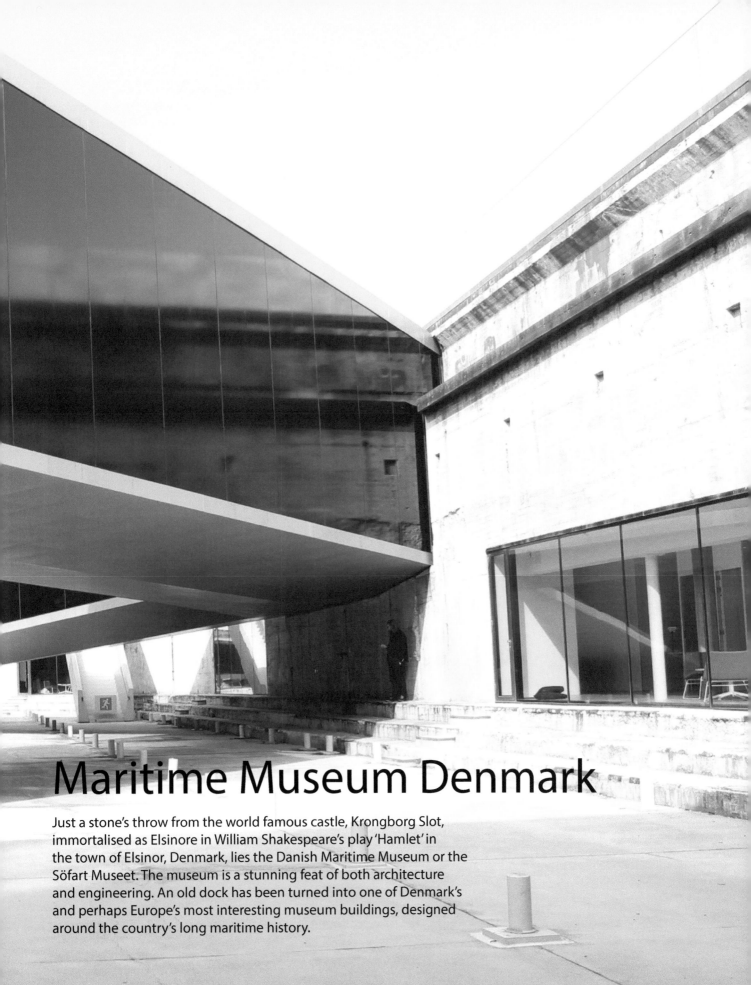

Maritime Museum Denmark

Just a stone's throw from the world famous castle, Krongborg Slot,
immortalised as Elsinore in William Shakespeare's play 'Hamlet' in
the town of Elsinor, Denmark, lies the Danish Maritime Museum or the
Söfart Museet. The museum is a stunning feat of both architecture
and engineering. An old dock has been turned into one of Denmark's
and perhaps Europe's most interesting museum buildings, designed
around the country's long maritime history.

From a distance, the museum is almost invisible. It is only close up that the sheer size and scale of the project become apparent. The base is a 125 year old (harbour) dry dock. The dock's old concrete walls have been given an ultra modern criss cross design with glass and aluminium clad bridges and stairs. The overall impression to the visitor is of a dramatic and intriguing vista.

A gently sloping staircase leads the visitor down into an underground world.

The first official documents mentioning Helsingör date as far back as 1231. In 1585, the imposing renaissance castle of Krongborg had just been completed. It was very much intended to be a defensive castle acting as a deterrent for any hostile vessels that might have been passing through Öresund, on their way to and from the Baltic, Helsingör being the closest point. By then Denmark was well on its way to becoming one of the world's leading seafaring nations, a position it holds to this day.

The Helsingör Skibsvaerft (shipyard) and machine factory was founded in 1882 and both were to play an important role in the subsequent industrialisation of the city.

The museum dock was built in 1892. It was constructed eight meters below ground level and was 3000 sqm and 150 m long; the measurements corresponded with those of a ship.

Building downwards instead of up and rising high, the architects Bjarke Ingels and David Zahle and their team, have designed the museum with more than a nod towards the long history of one of the important ship building docks of Helsingör.

Rather than opting for some spectacular 'sky-scraper' type design, as so often seen in the current architectural climate, the team has instead, chosen to add contemporary elements in order to emphasise the dry dock's past and it's original purpose, the construction of big ships and their subsequent maintenance.

The dock is kept in place by 461 ground anchors; these are fixed at a depth of 42 metres underground. Without the anchors, water pressure would simply push the museum building upwards and make it 'float' (much like a ship!) above the water level.

Given that the building is a museum below sea level, it has required extraordinary structural engineering, of a kind never before seen in Denmark. The project has evolved into a remarkable building; the marriage of a building which is more than a century old and contemporary design is truly spectacular.

The interiors of the Söfart museum provide an interesting and exciting odyssey through maritime history. Permanent exhibitions provide the visitor with amazing insights into the world of seafaring, both then and now. Wonderful visual effects bring alive the dramatic events of the past, pleasure cruising, technical information, memorabilia, economic issues and international trade history. And right down on the lowest level is the café/restaurant, which has been thoughtfully designed using materials and colours to match the building itself. This has perhaps one of the most interesting views onto the old dock and its ultra-modern additions.

www.mfs.dk

WHAT	Savoy Restaurant
WHEN	1937
WHERE	Helsinki, Finland
WHO	Alvar Aalto (1898 – 1976)
	Aino Aalto (1894 – 1949)

Savoy Restaurant

The Southern Esplanade in Helsinki is located in the heart of the city with beautiful old buildings lining the Esplanade. A luxury commercial centre and a renowned location for Finnish business and financial transactions, make the Southern Esplanade hot, happening and always in fashion.

The Savoy Restaurant is THE place to be seen, eat and drink, celebrate weddings or anniversaries, as well as discuss business strategy over lunch, Soon to celebrate its 80th birthday, the Savoy was designed and decorated by the famous architect couple Alvar and Aino Aalto.

When the Savoy building was inaugurated in 1937, one of it's most talked about feature was the four high speed elevators. Stepping out on the seventh floor leads directly to the Savoy Restaurant foyér. The original glass vases from Alvar Aalto's famous series, which he described as resembling "an Eskimo woman's leather trousers", are on a shelf on one of the walls; this is design history in its most expressive and, unprecedentedly futuristic form.

The original vase, which is still in production in littala, was designed for the glass factory there and created for the Paris exhibition 1936.

It became a design sensation when the Aaltos used the vases to decorate the restaurant tables in 1937.

Restaurant reviewers have said that the length of the Savoy recalls the sleek elegance of a classic Pullman railway carriage or, the first class dining room of a functionalist Atlantic liner from the 30's.

Both analogies are probably a good way to describe the style and design. During the functionalist decade, architects and designers were, to a fairly great extent, inspired by speed, aerodynamics and a certain laid back elegance.

The Savoy pays homage to Finnish-Swedish gentility; this gentility is paired with bourgeois stability and a hint of 'don't touch'. The owners (who run a chain of Finnish restaurants) have taken pride in retaining the interior and the furniture in the forms of the original era.

Everything is exactly as it looked on the inauguration day in 1937, despite the obviously necessary renovations that have been carried out over the years to keep the elegant fixtures and fittings in top condition.

Old established Helsinki families meet here to celebrate, parents, children, grandchildren and relatives. Leading industrialists discuss business arrangements over lunch and for international celebrities, dining here is a must.

Aino and Alvar Aalto worked closely together on the interior furniture, lighting, textiles and objects. Renowned design partners included textile artist Dora Jung and the furniture company Artek, where the then young Aaltos were co-founders (1935) together with Maire Gullichsen and Nils-Gustav Hahl.

The furniture is classically understated, the lighting from the polished brass lamps discreet - the roof lamp, the Golden Bell is still in production - and the starched linen tablecloths are dazzling white.

The curvaceous design of the chairs is elegant and ergonomically comfortable; they are covered in a sombre dark blue textile.

Long leather sofas line one wall, recalling a classic French bistro interior, where guests can sit in a row with a great view over the rest of the restaurant and other diners.

The table originally used by the famous Field Marshall Mannerheim, Finland's great WW2 hero and first Finnish president, still stands at the end of this long row of sofas.

Mannerheim was a regular at the Savoy. His favourite dish was the so called Vorsmack; a renowned mixture of beef and lamb, anchovies, onion, garlic, tomato puree, stock and white pepper. The dish's origins are Polish and it is served with baked potatoes, pickles and beetroot.

Legend has it that during the war, the windows of the restaurant, facing the street below Mannerheim's table, were covered with heavy drapes. This meant the enemy snipers, for whom Mannerheim was a prize target, could not get a clear shot and the Marshall could eat his lunch in peace!

www.savoy.fi
www.iittala.fi
www.artek.fi

WHAT Vignamaggio
WHEN Early 1500's
WHERE Greve in Chianti, Tuscany, Italy

Vignamaggio

Legend has it that the world famous 'Mona Lisa'
was a portrait of the young Italian noblewoman,
Monna Lisa Gherardini or 'La Giconda' and was
painted at the Vignamaggio vineyard near
Greve in Chianti in Tuscany.

The estate has a magnificent park and dates from the early 14th century. It is a graceful interpretation of early Renaissance architecture and garden styles.

Over six centuries of searing summer heat and fierce northern 'tramontana' winds have polished the Vignamaggio facades into a pale shade of pinkish grey. The overall impression is graceful and easy-going, yet with an almost 'fairytale' like quality. Think of a glass of cool sophisticated rosé wine, set amidst stately cypress trees and manicured boxwood hedges.

It is easy to visualise the Italian nobility of days gone by strolling in the gardens, engaged in courtship rituals and contests, laughing and joking together; a veritable garden of Eden for the most privileged members of society.

The estate is set in between Firenze and Siena, in the midst of the world famous Chianti wine growing region. The earliest documents referring to wine production at Vignamaggio, date back to 1404.

Life was harsh at this time; instability was a part of life. Land with fertile soil and in strategic positions was highly sought after by those who wanted to expand their estates and holdings. Marriage was one way to acquire land but more aggressive tactics were also used and minor wars between the landed nobility were far from uncommon.

The Gherardini family's ancestral seat was Montagliari castle. After years of suffering from problems with both debt and attacks by rival families, they were eventually hounded out of Montagliari and settled down at the Vignamaggio estate.

During the 1400's the Gherardinis were, once again, able to create a family empire due to the social and economic development opportunities that the era offered, which counterbalanced the instability of the time. Vignamaggio was improved and extended and became an elegant Renaissance mansion set amidst vineyards, rolling Tuscan hills, cypress trees and golden wheat fields.

Unfortunately, fresh family conflicts and disputes over land and money saw the Gherardinis become fugitives in their own lands. History had repeated itself. In 1421 close relatives, the Gherardini, managed to purchase Vignamaggio.

As time passed, relationships between the two rival families seem to have improved as it is here

at Vignamaggio, that we find the young Monna Lisa Gherardini visiting her cousins during the late 1400s.

Between 1503 and 1506 Leonardo da Vinci produced his portrait of a young Italian noblewoman. The woman's expressions are both sensual and enigmatic, roguish and yet maternal. The identity of the subject has been debated down the centuries and various theories have been expounded. Is it a self-portrait by the artist? Is it his mother? Is it a member of the nobility, perhaps Caterina Sforza, the princess Isabel of Aragon? The speculations are endless.

However, there is clear evidence that da Vinci visited Vignamaggio as a guest on several occasions. We cannot discount the theory that he met Monna Lisa Gherardini here and was charmed by her outstanding beauty and in the middle of the 17th century, the portrait was identified by the historian and artist Georgio Vasari as being Monna Lisa Gherardini (1479-1542), married to Franscesco del Giaconda. Hence the enigmatic nickname 'La Gioconda'.

Stories that have grown up around Vignamaggio and the painting of the Mona Lisa, state that Leonardo had a studio, a very small north facing room where 'La Gioconda' is said to have posed for her portrait.

The view from this window is identical with that of the background in the portrait. Whilst this legend is fascinating, it is also questionable and does not provide any clear evidence as to the identity of the

sitter. Equally, more modern research has sugge-
sted that the woman in the portrait may very well
be Monna Lisa Gherardini.

The gardens in Vignamaggio were overhauled in
the 1930's to recreate Renaissance ideals of sym-
metry, elegance, order, beauty and balance.
Slender cypresses stand to attention along well
manicured boxwood edged garden paths. Sculptures of lions, ancient gods, scantily clad god-
desses atop plinths and snarling mythical beasts
along with busts, fountains, ponds, terraces and
parterres, give Vignamaggio it's classical Renaissance character. Hand-forged iron grills still cover
the windows to deter unwanted intruders.

In one corner, stands a statue of Dante. Perhaps
his thoughtful features reflect his contemplation of
the follies of the time.

www.vignamaggio.com

WHAT   Bodegaz López de Heredia Vina Todonia
WHEN   2002
WHERE   Haro, La Rioja, Spain
WHO   Zaha Hadid (1950 – 2016)

"As a woman I´m expected to want everything to be nice and to be nice myself. A very English thing. I don´t design nice buildings – I dont like them. I like architecture to have some raw, vital, earthy quality"

Zaha Hadid

www. lopezheredia.com

Vina Tondonia

In 2002, the Spanish wine producers Lopez de Heredia were busy celebrating their 125th anniversary and decided that their presence at the annual wine and food trade show in Barcelona - the Alimentaria - would be the ideal opportunity to showcase a trade stand that would encompass both the ancient family traditions and the new departures in wine making in the region.

The architect Zaha Hadid was invited to design the Heredia pavilion at the fair and the Heredia trade stand has now been incorporated into the 'bodega', the wine boutique, which adjoins Heredia's existing buildings, some of which date from the 1870's

Since the mid 19th century some of the most important Spanish bodegas have been based in the city of Haro, in the northern Spanish province of La Rioja.
Haro is home to classic Spanish wines and was declared an historic site in 1975 due to its significant architecture importance and numerous ancient palaces. It was also the first city in Spain to get electric street lighting!

Wine producer Lopez de Heredia Vina Tondonia is among the oldest wine producers in the La Rioja area and the company was founded by the Chilean Don Rafael Lopéz de Heredia. Don Rafael built his first bodega in the 1870's and took a keen interest in the arts and architecture. The rural architectural style of the French region of Aquitaine, with its impressive farms and dovecotes, often built in the half timbered style, caught Don Rafael's interest.
The "Txoki Tori", or 'bird house' in Basque, became the bodega´s 'high rise' emblem; the name was placed on the top so that the brand was visible even at a distance.

The company was already an international name, when they took part in the world exhibition in Brussels back in 1910. For this fair, Lopez de Heredia commissioned a new publicity stand to promote their wines and it was designed in the then still fashionable, art noveau style, which was soon to be followed by the art dèco movement.
After the fair was over, the promotional stand was moved to Haro and the Lopez de Heredia Bodega, where it was dismantled and stored in the winery for almost a century.

To commemorate another jubilee, this time the company´s 125th anniversary in 2002, the family decided to add an entirely modern architectural twist to the old buildings. Perhaps

this decision was made to reflect the fact that the Rioja wine region already had begun to update both its old, conventional wine production methods and the architectural style of its bodegas. A new era had begun and commercial wine promotion needed to reflect that and emphasise the new wine making methods.

The (late) Anglo/Iranian architect, Zaha Hadid, attracted the family´s interest in their search for something utterly modern. They approached Hadid and she expressed interest in the family's suggestion that she take on the design of the new bodega.

Zaha Hadid decided to draw on an interpretation of a classic wine decanter shape, with a typically broad base and narrow neck. The result is a spectacular architectural 'bottle' shaped building with a soft rolling roof. At the family's request, she also left space for the ancient promotional stand to be reinstated; the then cutting edge design of the 1910 promotional stand from Brussels, now rubs shoulders with the remarkably modern new decanter shaped "Hadid bodega", which was completed in 2002.

The overall impression is of a significant show stopper. Whether you are a native of the city or on the wine tourist trail, you can't miss it, that was the architect's intention. The eye catching dichotomy between the ultramodern design and the older classical architecture is strikingly apparent and perfectly captures the family's desire to stress both their historical place in the world of wine

Italian Cultural Institute

When the Italian Culture Institute, designed by
Italian architect Gio Ponti, opened in november 1958,
it caused quite a stir among those in the arts world.

Sweden was preparing to start what was known as 'The Million program'; this was a giant experiment in social architectural building involving the construction of modern, repetitive, structured housing for thousands of the Swedish populace.

Ponti, the founder of the famous design magazine DOMUS, had gone out on a limb here, designing the Institute as an elegant and personal statement in a form of modern renaissance architecture.

The exterior is pure white (save for a later addition but this was in any case approved of by Ponti), and clad in white mosaic tiles. The building is extremely slim and low rise. This was in total contrast to the modernist skyscrapers that were being planned and executed for Swedish public buildings and housing projects at this time, when great swathes of the Stockholm city centre were being torn down to make way for new commercial buildings and offices, thus destroying the rich architectural heritage of the 17th and 18th centuries.

The construction of the new Institute was in the main, made possible due to a donation from the Italian industrialist C. M. Lerici, who was involved in trading with Sweden. The project was also sponsored by the Swedish king, Gustav VI Adolf, who was a keen amateur archaeologist and often took part in digs in Southern Italy.

Over the years, the Institute has acted as a cultural platform for lectures, concerts, films and exhibitions. Among many others, it has welcomed the likes of Pier Paolo Pasolini, Ingmar Bergman, Eugenio Montale and Sandro Chia and the Institute has arguably become an additional post war Italian 'embassy' in Sweden.

With the Institute Ponti created a very personal expression of airy architectural ease. The floating layouts of the interiors are divided by slim mural elements with sharp angles. The open, sparsely furnished rooms that feature throughout the interi-

or, reveal Ponti's love of clean interiors. The floors are all finished in light grey Carrara marble which reflects the movements of visitors to the Institute and thus creates an interplay of light and shade. There is a kind of classical fragile elegance and yet, at the same time, a typical interpretation of the 50's modernist movement in terms of form and colour.

Pieces of furniture, produced by Cassina and Chiesa, can still be found in the rooms and the textiles, lamps and all the items of furniture designed by Ponti, were made specially for the Institute.

The various differently shaped tables and shelves are covered in formica, sometimes in forms that could almost be termed frivolous. The armchairs and sofas, covered in synthetic leather, recall Italian public building interiors and offices from the 40's and 50's.

Windows are often dressed with timber shelving surrounds for books and art. The thin walls are movable and the lighting is often built in for special effects.

Ponti's famous Superleggia chair, was designed for Cassina at the same time as the Institute and original models from that era can be found here en masse.

The Institute stands in the same area as many embassy buildings in Stockholm, (the Gärdet area); other interesting architectural neighbours include buildings such as the Swedish Film Institute by Swedish Peter Celsing (1968) and the Finnish embassy (2001) by Kristian Gullichsen.

www.iicstoccolma.esteri.it

WHAT	Maison Louis Carré
WHEN	1956-1959/1963
WHERE	Bazoches-sur-Guyonne, France
WHO	Alvar Aalto (1898 – 1976)

Maison Louis Carré

The streets of the small village of Bazoches-sur-Guyonne near Paris, are lined with fairytale houses, many with thatched roofs, carefully manicured gardens and walls built in golden limestone. It is a scene that could well be found in many rural settings in southern England or even Brittany. So, it is perhaps even more surprising to discover in the vicinity of the village and hidden on the border of the Rambouillet forest, between Versailles and Chartres, Maison Louis Carré, a spectacular modernist villa.

industrialist Harry Gullichsen and his wife Marie in 1939) and other Aalto buildings. Shortly after, Alvar and Elissa Aalto came to France to visit the site. The location of the building plot was decided on, as was the shape and form of the roof. Carré was certain that he did not want a flat roof, and Aalto agreed that a sloping roof would blend in better with the landscape. Other than that, Aalto was given almost free rein in terms of the rest of his design.

In autumn 1957, the final plans were completed and construction began.

Elissa Aalto (1922-1994), Aalto's second wife, supervised the project and spent long periods of time in France. Alvar Aalto also visited the building site regularly himself. Having participated in the design process in Finland, the Swiss architect Marlaine Perrochet oversaw the on-site construction and took on particular responsibility for the interiors.

This private villa, built in the later half of the 1950's, was commissioned by the Parisian art dealer Louis Carré and designed by Finnish architect Alvar Aalto.

Louis Carré and Alvar Aalto met at the Venice Biennale in 1956, where Aalto was responsible for the Finnish pavilion. The famous architect and the respected gallerist were from the same generation and shared many ideas on architecture, the art and design of their time and its ideals. Indeed, as Carré explained, "We had both a rather universal idea of art".

In 1955, Louis Carré bought 21 farmland plots in Bazoches with the intention of building a home for himself and his wife. This was also going to be a place where he could put his collection on display. He initially thought of using Le Corbusier, whom he knew well. However, Le Corbusier's preference for concrete buildings made him change his mind in favour of Alvar Aalto.

After the meeting in Venice, Louis Carré went to Finland and visited the Villa Mairea (built for the

The building is situated at the top end of a three hectare plot and in no way detracts from the sloping landscape. The ground floor centers around the large entrance hall and can be divided into three main zones. These are the 'public' area which includes the hall, living room, library and dining room, the 'private' area comprising a sauna and three bedrooms, all with en-suite bathrooms, and the 'service' area which contains the kitchen, pantry and staff dining room. There are staff bedrooms and a linen room on the first floor and the basement houses the boiler room and a wine cellar.

Despite not being excessive in size (350 m2 on the ground floor and 90 m2 on the first floor) the property possesses remarkable qualities of both space and organisation.

The main entrance is situated on the north side of the building, the kitchen and the service areas on the east. The living room and the library face west with a view of the garden and the surrounding landscape; the bedrooms and bathrooms face south. Each important room also has it own external space; the living room and library open onto a terrace and the lawn, the bedrooms and bathrooms onto private terraces sheltered by brick and timber walls.

These terraces are invisible from the access part as well as from the rest of the garden, thanks to the broken perspective created by the turf stairs. This provides the occupant with complete privacy – an example of Aalto´s constant attention to the comfort of those who use his buildings.

When entering the main hall, the wooden vault creates a striking effect, towering initially at a height of five meters before bowing softly towards the steps that lead to the living room. This ceiling, a strongly emphasised feature of Aalto design, is the only free-form element and it creates a sense of width and space throughout the entire house. The lighting, both natural and artificial, comes from the skylights above the main door as well as from three large hanging lamps, all of which emphasise the impression of an open and generous space.

As with the exterior, interior materials have been carefully chosen. Finnish red pine was used for the hall and living room ceilings and in the sitting room where it was even laid by Finnish joiners. Other materials include oak parquet flooring and shelving in the library, ash and teak doors, frames and fittings with bronze and leather handles.

Much of the furniture, lighting and textiles were designed specially for the villa and other pieces were chosen from the Artek catalogues (Artek was founded in 1935 to manufacture and spread Aalto's design).
The entire project was aimed at creating a feeling of discrete and luxurious comfort.

Alvar Aalto also designed the exterior environment, including the access, garage and garden. The garden is composed of free form lawned spaces, a small wooded area, asymmetrical steps and a small amphitheatre. There was originally a small vineyard placed close to the house (now no longer) and once the Carrés had moved in, Aalto continued to add elements such as exterior lighting,

www.maisonlouiscarre.fr

flagpoles and most importantly, the swimming pool and pool house, completed in 1963.

Maison Louis Carré can be compared to Aalto's other large residence, the Villa Mairea, built in Noormarkku (Finland) some twenty years earlier, in 1938-39. Both houses share some similarities in that they were commissioned by wealthy art patrons who encouraged their architect with great freedom in terms of the initial design and end result.
However, whereas the Finnish villa was an experimental work which underwent numerous changes during the construction process, Maison Carré is a work of maturity with great structural, stylistic and material consistency. From the first sketches in 1956 until completion in 1959, the plans and interiors underwent only a very few modifications.

Louis Carré lived in his house until his death in 1977. During his lifetime, many important guests visited Bazoches. Among many others, these included the artists Marcel Duchamp and Juan Miro, the writer Paul Eluard, famous actors such as

Madeleine Renaud and her husband Jean-Louis Barrault and politicians including the Finnish president Urho Kekkonen. Annual garden parties also drew hundreds of guests to the villa.
Olga Carré stayed on in the house until she passed away in 2002.

Maison Louis Carré was listed as a 'Monument Historique' in 1996 and was purchased by the 'Alvar Aalto en France' foundation in 2006, whose stated purpose is: "The purchase and administration of the Maison Louis Carré at Bazoches-sur-Guyonne in view of promoting public interest and culture as well as the history and work of Finnish architect Alvar Aalto".

Finn Juhl's House

Danish architect Finn Juhl should be considered one
of the modern mid century's greatest Danish aesthetes.
He is the first recognised architect to put Denmark on
the international design map after the second world war.
He was THE designer to be first associated with the
expression 'Danish Modern' in USA.

WHAT   Finn Juhl's House
WHEN   1942
WHERE   Ordrupsgaard Museum Copenhagen, Denmark
WHO   Finn Juhl (1912 – 1989)

"Finn Juhls house is a one of refinement and simpleness, not without the influence of a certain japanese elegance"

Finn Juhl started to design furniture in the 1930's. He attended 'Kunstakademiets Arkitektskole' in Copenhagen between 1930-34 under the tutorship of architect Kay Fisker.

Juhl founded his own architectural studio in 1945. As a furniture designer he was self-taught and eventually also became very well known for his consumer goods in glass and teak which are both elegant and user-friendly.

In 1942, Juhl took delivery of his own brand new house at Kratvaenget 18 in Charlottenlund near Copenhagen. The house is an early example of open plan architecture; Juhl felt it was vital to be able see from room to room. The large 270 meter square house consists of two parallel buildings. It was designed 'inside-out'; with clever draftsmanship Juhl managed to get the facades of the house to follow the interiors which were designed first around the furniture. This 'inside and out' philosophy is used today as a model for user based innovation in modern industrial design.

There is a harmonious feeling to the rooms. Several pieces of furniture are placed in intimate groups, whether for entertaining, resting, eating, working or sleeping, many of which interact in one big space. White-washed timber plank flooring creates a warm and natural feeling in all the rooms; this is a typical Danish tradition, seen in both old farm houses and mansions.

Every piece of furniture was designed by Juhl himself, many of them in cooperation with the skillful furniture maker Niels Vodder. The overall effect is a harmonious blend of sculptural and curvaceous elements.

The inclusion of a certain Japanese influenced elegance means that Finn Juhl's house is both refined and simple.

www.ordrupgaard.dk

WHAT   Sao Lourenco do Barrocal, Farm Estate retreat
WHEN   200 years ago, newly renovated
WHERE   Alentejo, Portugal
WHO   Developer José António Uva / Eduardo Souto de Moura

Barrocal
– a visionary luxury "farm retreat" in Alentejo

Alentejo, is awash with trees, olive trees, cork oaks, lemon and orange trees and the hilltops are dotted with small villages covered in white washed houses. This is an unspoiled part of Portugal, and is, in fact on of the least populated parts of southern Europe.

Alentejo is around one and a half hours from Lisbon and close to the Spanish border.

If you inherited an ancient and very run down farm, the size of an entire village plus 780 hectares of land, what would you do? This is the question that perplexed José Antonio Uvas when he inherited the 200 year old family farm, the Sao Lorenco do Barrocal.

In days gone by the farm had been home to around 50 people and was entirely self-contained, producing its own food, wine and olive oil. There was a school, a church, a communal bread oven and even a bullring.

It took José nearly eight years to decide what to do with the farm. Eight years of planning, working on the project and finding like minded people to support his vision, and today, the giving the farm a new lease of life has become José's lifelong work.

The road that leads to the farm is a simple sandy track, and as we drive along, we throw up heavy clouds of dust. As we pass through the flat land covered with cork oaks, we encounter herds of long-horned cows and horses and riders.

We arrive at the parking place and discover that cars are not allowed to any further, but almost immediately, an electric powered golf cart arrives, and we are invited to climb aboard with our bags.

On the way to the farm we had already noticed the remarkable large boulders that dot the terrain and when we stopped at reception to collect some maps and information on the area, we were told that these date from the Neolithic period! We decide to borrow bicycles and explore the area.

Inside the hotel the rooms are spacious. Our bathroom is also an extremely good size and

we have a terrace. The entire interior has a natural feel and all the furniture, leather chairs and textiles are made by local craftsmen.

The farm has been given a new lease of life and once again, produces its own wine and olive oil. There is a bar, restaurant, shop and spa for guests and you can also go horse riding and cycling.

www.barrocal.pt

Café Iruna

Standing in the bar area of the legendary Café Iruna in Bilbao, one cannot but admire the interiors which are over one hundred years old. Café Iruna is THE meeting place for pinxtos aficionados and is equally renowned as an extremely classy meeting place where locals gather to gossip and chat.

WHAT	Café Iruna
WHEN	1903
WHERE	Bilbao, Spain
WHO	Severo Unzue Donamariá

- "Do you like the interiors?", asks the elegant woman seated at the table next to ours.
She has obviously overheard our conversation, even if it is being conducted in a foreign language, and registered the photographer's relentlessly clicking camera.
- "Yes", we reply, "we have visited a couple of times and we are fascinated by this place."
- "Well, you know, my grandfather built this place." What a coincidence!

Café Iruna was opened in 1903. A wine merchant named Severo Unzue Donamariá originating from the Navarre region, had made a small fortune in the wine business, when he decided to open the café and quickly became a respected member of Bilbao society. This was, no doubt, due in no small part to the fact that the café Iruna instantly became one of the most frequented cafés/restaurants in Bilbao; a position which it still retains today.

It was new, it was stylish, it was art nouveau and took much of its inspiration from Moorish decorative schemes with its ornamental arabesque design and colour palette; one of the great design trends of the era.

Huge ceramic tiles on the walls, advertising the (then) most famous and up to date wine and liquor companies of the era create an incredibly striking effect in the bar.

At the beginning of the 20th century, Bilbao was a booming commercial and industrial city in the north of Spain where big money ruled and fortunes could be made. The period known as 'La Belle Époque' was at its peak; optimism and economic prosperity reigned supreme.

The magnificent avenues and boulevards of Bilbao which today are still lined with beautifully well preserved and maintained art nouveau buildings, were all being developed, so, what was more appropriate, than to gather together the very latest trends in architecture and interior design in the Café Iruna.

Everybody who was somebody in Bilbao was frequently spotted here, wealthy tradespeople, aristocratic families, politicians, industrialists, artists and most probably the Bilbao demi-monde, the slightly 'edgy' women of the era who were plied with lavish gifts and cash from their current lovers, and who would keep this elegant crowd of wealthy pleasure seekers entertained.

The Café Iruna has retained its authentic atmosphere. It is friendly rather than snobbish, inexpensive yet luxurious and above all, has a joyful friendly atmosphere especially in the evenings.

The luxurious feeling that stems from the surroundings and somewhat glitzy décor has not changed over time. It is like a perpetual gala; one that takes place every day, with the glittering chandeliers reflected in the colourful tiles, the original brass detailing and the enormous oval zinc bar countertop.

Restaurant guests are seated next to each other on long velvet covered benches or on original art nouveau chairs. Intricate columns, decorated with colourful tiles, support the ornate timber roof.

The walls are painted in a mix of both bright and sober colours and the floor is covered with Moorish inspired matt ceramic tiles. A dining area on the first floor is designed to resemble a huge opera box, where guests can catch sight of those dining downstairs.

Both lunch and dinner are served late, to suit the Spanish custom of eating out later in the day, and see the artfully composed still lives of pinxtos become an extraordinary, giant starter, hastily swept away by hungry guests, with wine glasses in hand.

Regulars and a younger crowd of workers from nearby offices as well as tourists, study the inexpensive lunch menus, which include wine.

During peak times, there might be a longer wait but this is made entirely bearable by a glass or two of the slightly sparkling local white Txakoli wine which comes from the Basque vineyards of Biscay.

www.cafeirunabilbao.net

Lightning Source UK Ltd.
Milton Keynes UK
UKHW050944090223
416724UK00003B/234

* 9 7 8 1 9 1 5 6 6 2 1 1 8 *